W0010527

Native

NATIVE

LIFE IN A VANISHING LANDSCAPE

PATRICK
LAURIE

BIRLINN

For my parents

First published in Great Britain in 2020 by
Birlinn Ltd
West Newington House
10 Newington Road
Edinburgh
EH9 1QS
www.birlinn.co.uk

ISBN: 978 1 78027 620 5

British Library Cataloguing-in-Publication Data
A catalogue record for this book is available
on request from the British Library

Typeset by Biblichor Ltd, Edinburgh
Printed and bound by Clays Ltd, Elcograf S.p.A.

Blows the wind to-day, and the sun and the rain are flying,
Blows the wind on the moors to-day and now,
Where about the graves of the martyrs the whaups are crying,
My heart remembers how!

Grey recumbent tombs of the dead in desert places,
Standing stones on the vacant wine-red moor,
Hills of sheep, and the howes of the silent vanished races,
And winds, austere and pure!

Be it granted me to behold you again in dying,
Hills of home! And to hear again the call;
Hear about the graves of the martyrs the peewees crying;
And hear no more at all.

Robert Louis Stevenson
Vailima, Samoa (1894)

CONTENTS

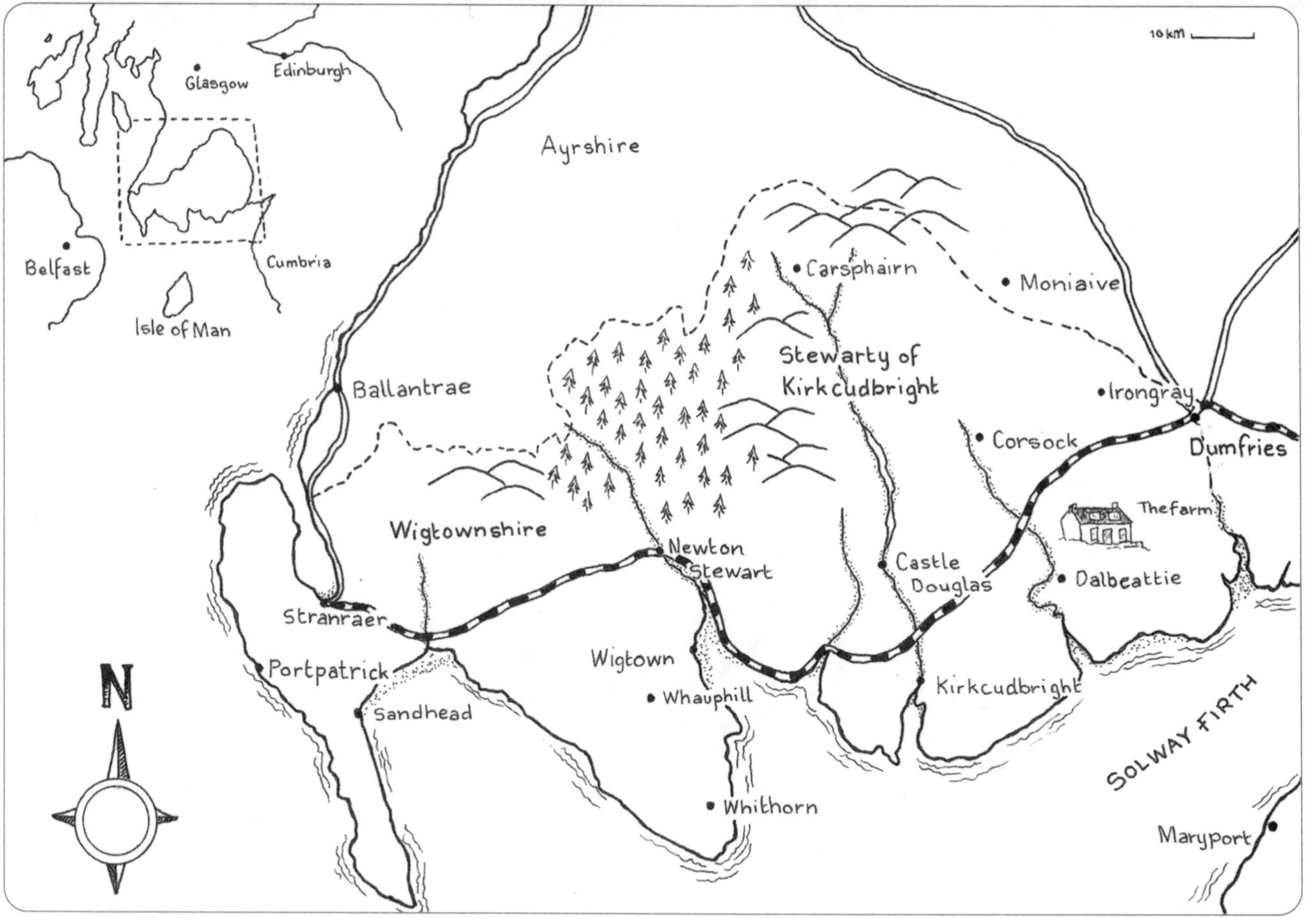
10 km
Glasgow
Edinburgh
Belfast
Cumbria
Isle of Man
Ayrshire
Ballantrae
Carsphairn
Moniaive
Stewarty of
Kirkcudbright
Irongray
Corsock
Dumfries
The farm
Wigtownshire
Newton
Stewart
Castle
Douglas
Dalbeattie
Stranraer
Portpatrick
Wigtown
Whauphill
Kirkcudbright
Sandhead
SOLWAY FIRTH
Whithorn
Maryport
N

Galloway

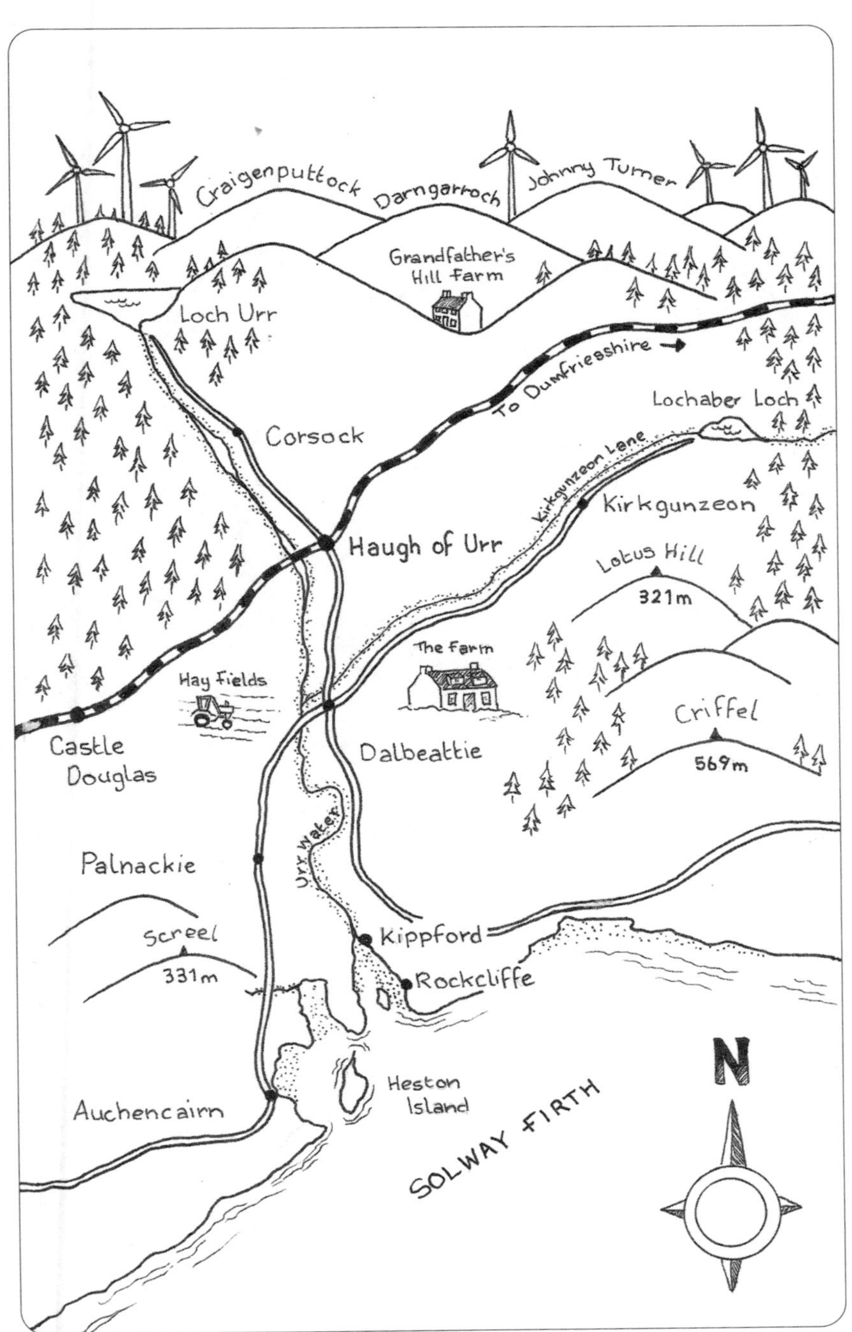

The Farm and Surrounding Area

BEGINNINGS

Winter Solstice – the Shortest Day

I peer through an open window in the darkness. The morning feels warm, and the fields click and chatter as they drain the night's rain. Drips plop off gutters in the yard and a curlew calls. Our cockerel answers from the shed, and his din makes the tin roof ring.

Curlews vanished from the glen when the weather was cold, but they returned within hours of the thaw. Large winter flocks come inland from the sea and probe the sodden ground with long, curved beaks. I take the dogs out before breakfast and find the half-light filled with the sound of wading birds.

Our stretch of the river was straightened many years ago. Men dug a new and more efficient path for the water, but they failed to iron out the old bends. The river follows a straight and perfect line through the dark soil, but you can still see where the old stream used to play in swampy, tangled loops. Heavy rain can bring this waterway back to life – subtle contours flood again and become strings of narrow pools, pouchy old veins which bristle with reeds. The new river rushes water briskly out to sea. The old one hoards the rain and refuses to let go.

Curlews cluster in these haunted, sodden corners. The dogs flush them as the day brightens, and they wail in the falling rain. Drainage pipes were buried across these fields to bail water into the river, but after years of service they are beginning to fail. The terracotta tiles are breaking and the water has started to flow backwards. Without human intervention, the river will begin to resume its ancient course – the curlews pray for it.

The new bull calf bellows when he hears me open the back door after breakfast. His shed is across the yard, and he listens to every move we make. He was timid and small when he arrived here on the lorry from Kendal. He sorely missed his mother, but now he is growing in confidence and roars to be fed. Dull days and low cloud reduce him to a dark silhouette in a pool of straw. There are no electric lights in this shed, but we can make out that he has a fine head. It is heavy and square like a Belfast sink, and the curls grow so thickly upon it that they swallow my fingers to the knuckle. I rub his brow and stir up delicious scents of sweat and dry grass. His blue tongue rasps at my cuff and I turn to stare out through the open doorway. I am seeing the world from his perspective and realise that this rectangular hole is like a cinema screen to him. He lurks in the gloom and the days purr by in a flick-book of still images, alternating phases of blue, grey and darkness. He watches endless repeats of wild swans on the bottom fields. Owls star in his nights.

Everyone agrees that he'd be better outdoors. This animal was bred for wide open spaces, but I have no other options and there are some advantages to this early confinement. He might roll his eyes and moan but he can settle here without coming to harm, and he can get to know us. Buying him was a gamble, and now I'm relieved to feel it paying off. It is hard to tell how a calf will be as an adult, but this lad has promise.

A starling dies at noon. I watch the falcon peeling the corpse from the kitchen window as I fry an egg. The day is already over and the fields begin to recede beneath a veil of thin, chesty cloud. Later I will find most of the starling's skull amongst a mess of feathers. It is a glossy ball which reminds me of a cape gooseberry; a discarded garnish.

Night falls with a rush of wildfowl. Ducks whoop in the deep blue, and the shapes of birds flare over the yard as I chop firewood. Then there is swirling rain which dances like smoke in the light of the kitchen window and lacquers the granite setts of the yard. It is only four thirty and a vixen is screaming for attention on the moss. The dogs cough to respond for a moment, then they jostle past my knees and back to the hot stove.

From this distance, summer feels like another place. I can hardly remember the sun, but now the darkening has slipped into reverse. Months of gradual compression will begin to relax, and daylight will leak back into our lives. It will be weeks before human beings can register the lengthening days, but the shift has been clocked by others. This wet, draining place is on the move at last.

*

Galloway is unheard of. This south-western corner of Scotland has been overlooked for so long that we have fallen off the map. People don't know what to make of us anymore and shrug when we try and explain. When my school rugby team travelled to Perthshire for a match, our opponents thumped us for being English. When we went for a game in England, we were thumped again for being Scottish. That was child's play, but now I realise that even grown-ups struggle to place us.

There was a time when Galloway was a powerful and independent kingdom. We had our own Gaelic language, and strangers trod carefully around this place. The Romans got a battering when they came here, and the Viking lord Magnus Barefoot had nightmares about us. In the days when longboats stirred the shallow broth of the Irish Sea, we were the centre of a busy world. We took a slice of trade from the Irish and sold it on to the English and the Manxmen who loom over the sea on a clear day. We spurned the mainstream and we only lost our independence when Scotland invaded us in the year 1236. Then came the new Lords of Galloway and the wild times of Archibald the Grim, and he could fill a whole book himself.

The frontier of Galloway was always open for discussion. Some of the old kings ruled everything from Glasgow to the Solway Firth, but Galloway finally settled back on a rough and tumbling core, the broken country which lies between tall mountains and the open sea. This was not an easy place to live in, but we clung to it like moss and we excelled on rocks and salt water both. We threw up standing stones to celebrate our paganism, then laid the groundwork for Christianity in Scotland. History made us famous for noble knights and black-hearted cannibals. You might not know what Galloway stands for, but it's plain as day to us.

We never became a county in the way that other places did. Galloway fell into two halves: Wigtownshire in the west and the Stewartry of Kirkcudbright in the east. There are some fine legal distinctions between a 'Shire' and a 'Stewartry', but that hardly matters anymore because both of them were deleted in 1975 when the local government was overhauled. The remnants of Galloway were yoked to Dumfries, and the result is a mess because Dumfries and Galloway are two very different things.

Dumfriesshire folk mistake their glens for dales and fail to keep Carlisle at arm's length. They're jealous of our wilderness and beauty, but we forgive them because it's unfair to gloat. Besides, they have the bones of Robert Burns to console them, and don't we all know it. Perhaps Dumfriesshire is a decent enough place, but we've pulled in different directions for too long to make an easy team. Imagine a county called 'Perth and Fife' or 'Carlisle and Northumberland'. Both would be smaller and more coherent than 'Dumfries and Galloway'. Now there are trendy councillors who abbreviate this clunky mouthful to 'D 'n' G', as if three small letters were enough to describe the 120 miles of detail and diversity which lie between Langholm and Portpatrick. Tourism operators say we are 'Scotland's best-kept secret', and tourists support that claim by ignoring us.

It's easy to see why visitors rarely come. They think we're just an obstacle between England and the Highlands. They can't imagine that there's much to see in the far south-west and tell us that 'Scotland begins at Perth'. Maybe it's because we don't wear much tartan, or maybe it's because we laugh at the memory of Jacobites and Bonnie Prince Charlie. Left to our own devices, we prefer the accordion to the pipes and we'd sooner race a gird than toss a caber. If you really want to see 'Scotland', you'll find it further north.

When Galloway folk speak of home, we don't talk of heather in bloom or the mist upon sea lochs and mountains. Our place is broad and blue and it smells of rain. Perhaps we can't match the extravagant *pibroch* scenery of the north, but we're anchored to this place by a sure and lasting bond. There are no wobbling lips or tears of pride around these parts; we'll leave that sort of carry-on to the Highlanders. We'll nod and make light of it, but we know that life away from Galloway is unthinkable.

My ancestors have been in this place for generations. I imagine them in a string of dour, solid Lowlanders which snakes out of sight into the low clouds. These were farming folk with southern names like Laidlaw and Mundell, Reid and Gilroy, and they worked the soil in quiet, hidden corners without celebrity or fame. Lauries don't have an ancestral castle to concentrate any feeling of heredity. We've worked in a grand sweep between Dunscore and Wigtown and now all of Galloway feels like it might've been home at one time or another. I was born to feel that there is only one place in this world, and I can hardly bear to spend a day away from it. Satisfaction alternates between quiet peace and raging gouts of dizzy joy.

Wild birds fly over Galloway. They move between the shore and the hills, and that journey brings them close at hand. I was brought up on a seaside farm where curlews spent their winter days in noisy gangs of a hundred and more. My father ran a mixed business based on sheep and beef cattle, and curlews flowed alongside him in rich furrows by the shore. When spring comes, curlews are blown uphill on warming winds to breed on the moors, and we followed them a few miles inland to pass many hours at work on my grandfather's hill farm. I heard the birds crying on busy days when the sheep were clipped and the peat was cut.

Unremarkable in flight, obscure in plumage and secretive to the point of rumour, curlews are unlikely heroes. But then they call over the shore and sing beneath the high-stacked clouds and there is nothing else of value. No other wild bird has that power to convey a sense of place through song. It's a grasping, bellyroll of belonging in the space between rough grass and tall skies, and you never forget it. The curlew's call became the year-long sound of my childhood. I hear that liquid, loving list and I'm lying in the warm, sheepy grass again, a small boy in too-big wellies, hugged by old familiar hills.

So I thought that curlews were mine. The connection was a livewire, but then I found that the birds had a place in all of us. My entire family would rush to the kitchen door at night to hear curlews passing between our chimney and the wide, dusty moon. We all loved them, so then I began to think that the birds belonged only to Galloway. In time I'd grow up and go elsewhere, and that's when I learned that curlews are loved by anybody who'll take the time to listen to them. People are devoted to curlews in Wales and Ireland, on Shetland and Exmoor; the birds have starred in heraldry, tradition and folklore for thousands of years. Everybody is tempted to claim the curlew, and no other bird can boast of such universal popularity.

I wrote about curlews as a teenager when my friends were smoking and chatting up girls. I hunted for more information about the birds through old school encyclopedias, but all I found were dry, papery sentences which were dull as wind-blown sinew. I went back to those words again and again, hoping that I could read some flesh onto the bare bones –

> **Curlew:** any of numerous medium-sized or large shorebirds belonging to the genus *Numenius* (family *Scolopacidae*) and having a bill that is decurved, or sickle-shaped, curving downward at the tip. Curlews are streaked, grey or brown birds with long necks and fairly long legs. They probe in soft mud for worms and insects, and they breed inland in temperate and sub-Arctic regions of the Northern Hemisphere.
>
> The common, or Eurasian, curlew (*N. arquata*), almost 60 cm (24 inches) long including the bill, is the largest European shorebird. This species breeds from Britain to Central Asia.

There was so little to go on. I began to write my own encyclopedia entries in the form of short descriptions and reports of encounters with the birds on the hill and the sea shore. I don't know what became of these projects – perhaps they have survived in jotters and folded pages stowed in the attic. It hardly matters, but the birds called me to stretch my legs and draw lines between known and unknown. Curlews were both, and I clung to them through adolescence and early adulthood. Their calls began to feature in tales of fumbling romance and the pressing growth of responsibility. They grew to fill more than just a blue-remembered childhood. I began to think they were an ever-present fact of life, as dependable as rain and moonlight.

Young people don't stay in Galloway. They go to Glasgow, and I went with them for a four-year stint at the university. The city was a clashing novelty, but then I graduated and found summer work on a Hebridean fishing boat. It was a dark morning on the bus from Buchanan Street to Uig, and rain lashed against the sweaty windows. An old Hebridean lady had made a fruit cake for the journey and passed it around the passengers as we slashed our way through Glen Coe. The work was a lunge at something different, and soon I was watching killer whales pass our small boat at dawn against the silhouette of Skye. Here was a fine place, but I was nagged by the knowledge that this was not my home. I didn't have the Gaelic, and I watched my friends at arm's length. They were born and raised on the Outer Isles, and I wondered how it would feel to have roots in that shallow, turquoise water. I was just paddling my toes in their world and I began to feel like a fraud. I envied the Dutch and German tourists who gawked at us on the jetty because they had nothing to prove.

The work also showed up my physical weakness and lack of stamina. I slobbered with tears and exhaustion after eighty-hour weeks, and I was forever shamed by the strength and power of men three times my age. We went over to Portree for a drink and one of the boys got into a fight. I was pathetic and fragile, and I ducked outside. There was crashing and swearing, and I growled on the harbour steps like a dog pretending to strain on its lead. I didn't want to fight, but it was galling to find that I couldn't if I tried. Soft-handed people like me often say that manliness doesn't matter anymore. We make it seem dumb and old-fashioned, but I grew up around capable, bull-necked men and there was no hiding from the shortfall. I said that I came back to Galloway because I had other plans. Weakness is closer to the truth.

And it was good to be home. Galloway poured back into my boots like peaty water, but it was hard to find solid footing in this place. I'd studied language and literature, but there wasn't much use for either in small towns where most of the shops are boarded up and jobs are hard to find. Our glory days are well behind us, and D 'n' G has slumped into decay. People say the best chance you've got of making money in Galloway is to buy a metal detector and spend your days hunting for your ancestors' gold.

I spent a few seasons drifting around south-west Scotland. I picked things up and replaced them again, I pulled pints and felled trees, and finally found some cash in freelance journalism. It paid the bills, but this line of work hardly carries much clout in a place where you're expected to have a one-word job title and you just get on with it. People asked 'what do you do these days'? I'd shrug and say 'all sorts', knowing that I'd fail to cut mustard.

My Cornish wife and I were married in the registry office in Glasgow. We'd met at university and we moved to a small cottage by the Solway shore where we could listen to curlews flying in the darkness. We assumed that our children would not be far away, but none came, so I leant back on married life with a shrug. Work was busy and time swirled past. I didn't mind the absence, and I felt sure that our family lay just around the corner. Years later, we'd recall this place during brusque interviews with a fertility specialist who asked us when we began 'trying' for a baby. It was in those days, but babies were one of many plans we had back then.

I returned to curlews in a loose, half-hearted kind of way. I liked the idea of writing a book about the birds, and the sudden collapse they've suffered over the last thirty years gave them a glaring relevance. We hardly need scientists to tell us that curlews have been declining across Britain over the last half-century. The birds used to be absurdly common, and now they are nearly gone. We've lost three-quarters of our curlews in Galloway since the 1990s, and some parishes have lost them all. I was old enough to have seen this collapse in real time. My nagging worries had become a constant ache; this is the latest disaster in a long and nationwide sequence of decline and collapse, but this one really hurts.

I began to examine curlews beneath a microscope. I gathered up mounds of scientific reports and started out on background reading, but the work was hard and I stumbled over the technical jargon. I'm no scientist; I had to launder ideas of ecosystems and biodiversity into something I could understand. People in Galloway aren't used to thinking about wild birds in isolation. They're part of something much bigger, and they hardly warrant anybody's full attention.

Visitors come and tell us that we live in a fine place to watch birds, but we've always taken our wildlife for granted.

Problems have only arrived here in the last few decades, and we've been spoiled by centuries of surplus. We've gorged on wild partridges and salmon for a thousand years, and now we are told to be careful with what we have because nature is fragile. True enough, our salmon have gone and our game is going, but we aren't sure what to make of birdwatchers and ecologists. They come from somewhere else and they usually tell us we're wrong.

I began to think that a book about curlews would've made no sense to my ancestors who'd farmed here and were preoccupied with soils and rain, beasts and grain. The birds were hardly worth noticing in the days of their prosperity, but now curlews have been transformed by their decline. They've become figures of tragedy to be studied in desperate detail. Everybody mourns the loss of curlews, but birds have always come naturally to us and we scratch our heads at this confusing failure.

I was besotted with birds. Curlews were my focus, but I'd often get up before dawn to watch black grouse and lapwings displaying in the rushes above the hill pens. I'm glad I made the time for those birds because they've all gone now. I knew the last black grouse by name, and I was there to see the final lapwing's egg. Curlews are the last of a grand dynasty of hill birds which has crumbled into ash during the short course of my life. My generation has arrived at a party which seems to be ending, and it's getting harder to recall birds as they were in the days of their plenty.

People often say that agriculture has driven this collapse. There's a long-running conflict between conservationists and farmers, and I was caught with a foot in both camps. Birdwatchers say that farmers don't give a damn about wildlife, but I couldn't square that with what I saw at home. My love of nature had always been egged on by my parents, who nudged and fired me up with their own stories and tales. My father used to bring me small treasures he'd found on the farm: I had an owl feather and a snake's skin on my bedside table. I was devoted to a dead mole which I carried everywhere in my jacket pocket for two weeks. I loved 'him' (or her) with desperate intensity, but this divine jewel went missing in mysterious circumstances. It took almost twenty years for me to realise that my parents had thrown the corpse away when it had finally sprung a leak and begun to melt.

My family was fascinated by nature, and many of our friends had an amazing wealth of knowledge about birds of all kinds. Some of these were hard-handed gamekeepers and deerstalkers who often slept on the open hill and knew magical details about rough grass and wide skies. They knew where to find deer kids in the bracken, and they watched the owls go down to roost. I gobbled up their stories and made them my own. I was just a boy, and I blurred the lines between truth and fiction.

I didn't realise that much of that wisdom was already muddled into mythology, and I swallowed it all without checking. I learned more about hen harriers from one old gamekeeper than I have from any book or study since, but the same man avidly believed in the craigie heron, a long-necked bird which prods for frogs by the light of the full moon. Craigie herons aren't magical or special beyond the realm of other birds; they just don't exist. But I believed in them like any kid would because the world is big and complicated, and I had no reason to suspect anything else.

Tales like these were ten a penny before the arrival of modern science. Galloway used to be full of tales about evil birds and lucky beasts, but now we have myth-busting experts working hard to break up that kind of nonsense. Ecologists say the worst thing you can do is muddle up fact and fiction, and they sneer that we didn't know much about wildlife until they arrived to set the record straight. And we don't like being laughed at, so we learn to keep old stories to ourselves. Maybe we suspect that we're behind the times, so we tuck our fictions away and let them wilt in darkness. It's getting harder to find native tales, particularly now there are structured, uniform ways to think about wildlife. Only children dally with magic, and we tell them the truth when they grow up.

I grew up and began to pull facts away from folklore. By an odd twist, it turned out that many of the real things were magical and much of the old superstition was dull. But if I wanted to write something credible about curlews, I would have to bend into new systems of taxonomy and binomial classification. This wasn't a good fit for me. Besides, I'd learned a great deal of truth from those ropey old stories. If nothing else, the sheer quantity of birdlore and gossip in circulation seemed to suggest that local people had a deep connection with the natural world. Following that thread, I couldn't sign up to the idea that farmers did not care about wildlife.

Drifting round my working world, I bumped into a small charity which promoted conservation in agriculture. I managed to find some work on a short-term project, and soon I'd found a grand overlap between farming and curlews. Managed correctly, farms can produce a wealth of wildlife, and human beings are a crucial part of that picture. My short-term project became a long-term job. I was assigned to follow some case studies where cattle were used to improve the land for curlews in Wales. Then I was asked to document a similar project in Perthshire. Over the course of several years I started to understand how the relationship works between food and wild birds. I travelled miles to stare at that buzz of goodness which flares up between cattle, humans and wildlife in Powys, Selkirk and Angus. I envied the farmers who were delivering results and were pumping new curlews into the sky every summer against the odds. These people didn't have advanced degrees or university jobs. They were normal folk like you and me, and I began to wonder if I could join them.

As a child, my sole ambition was to farm and raise livestock like my family had before me. I was gagging to pick up the baton and carry it forward, but the world intervened. Small farms had been trickling away for years, and 'mad cow disease' would quickly sink those who hadn't already jumped. Not long before my seventh birthday, my father crossed into the law and became a solicitor. His farm sank behind him and was gone. He leased the land to a series of tenants – bigger farmers who recognised that the only hope of survival lay in expansion.

My father's animals were loaded onto a lorry and vanished. The farm became something very different that day. Our fields lost their urgency and relevance. The hill had paid our bills, and now it was merely a place for walking dogs. If it rained, we stayed indoors. Our friends and neighbours fought hard to keep up with the changes in farming, but we were drifting away.

My grandfather was devoted to cattle. Sorely damaged by his time as a fighter pilot in the Battle of Britain, he could match the wildest bull for surliness and bad temper, but he was a superb stockman with a love for his animals. He'd finished the war with the rank of Group Captain, and this is how he was known to friend and foe until the end of his life. He died and left me with fond memories of a red-faced and desperately powerful man in a husky jacket. I thought that his rosy complexion was the product of a robust outdoor life, but

I later found that his skin had been seared away in the cockpit of a burning Spitfire as it plummeted into the streets of Wanstead half a century before.

Some of my earliest memories are of visiting his cows at the local agricultural shows. He'd devoted his life to a kind of beast which has deep roots in local history and culture, and his 'Galloways' picked up rosettes in Wigtown and Castle Douglas. We think of Scottish beef and conjure up images of windswept red Highlanders with long horns and fluttering fringes, but Galloways are the driving heroes of Lowland farming from Stranraer to Duns. My grandfather's cattle were jet-black, curly-haired beasts with square, hornless heads and fluffy ears. To outsiders it will seem like a modest claim to fame, but these animals are the finest product that Galloway has ever delivered to the world.

My mother would take me to see my grandfather's cattle as they lay on beds of fresh straw in the show lines. His farm name was painted on a board which hung above the cows, and the thick-wristed stockmen would wink at me and grin through a haze of cigarette smoke because I was the Group Captain's grandson. We no longer had cattle at home, but here was a crucial thread of contact with heavy beasts. I don't remember the animals so well as the paraphernalia which surrounded them – brushes, combs, nets of hay and coils of rope. Results from the judging were recited deadpan across a crackling tannoy: beasts from Rusko and Glaisters, from Barlay and Barcloy, from Plascow and Congeith. I was a small child, and these farm names plotted a complete map of the known universe. Here were my uncles and cousins, friends and family from far-flung places across the Southern Uplands, each with their own Galloway cattle as if no other breed existed. Even at this primal stage and divorced from animals of our own, my life was in orbit around beef.

Galloway has given its name to a breed of cattle, but so has Hereford, Devon and Sussex. There was a time when almost every county or region in Britain had its own breed. Dramatic changes during the twentieth century put paid to many of those old animals, and several weren't deemed profitable in a modern farmyard. Agriculture was intensifying and animal breeding began to specialise on growth, scale and speed. We said goodbye to Sheeted Somerset cattle, the Suffolk Dun and the Caithness cow, as well as more than twenty other breeds of British livestock between 1900 and 1973. Galloways almost collapsed, and the old animals were replaced by fast-growing bulls from France and Belgium; heavy-lifters with strange and unpronounceable names. Most of the surviving native breeds were reduced to obscurity, just hobby projects for quirky smallholders and stubborn old folk.

But every native breed excels at something special. Tamworth pigs make superb bacon; Gloucester cattle produce milk which cheesemakers adore. Native breeds represent a wide variety of traits, characteristics and flavours which took centuries to refine. High-octane European breeds might have maximised productivity, but this has come at a cost to variety. Our food has been subverted by monotony.

Galloway cows have a particular knack for digesting rough grass. They're born hungry, and they'll fatten on feed which many other breeds would refuse to sleep on. A summer heifer fills herself with roughage until she's as thick and fat as a grand piano, and the grass goes to build sweet, fine-grained beef. The muscle is laid down slowly, and the flavour is matched with a fine, melting texture. The sixteenth-century scholar Hector Boece praised Galloway beef as 'right delicius and tender', and modern chefs are titillated by T-bones and rib-eyes which are sold in the best and most exclusive restaurants across Britain. Like many native livestock breeds, Galloway cattle still exist because some people are prepared to pay more for food which 'tastes like it used to'.

The Galloway's reputation for superb beef is countered by rumours of violence and awkwardness. In the old days, cattle were cast into the hills and recovered to be killed after four years. These semi-feral beasts grew up to be cunning and insincere. It's not so long ago that a friend of my grandfather's was sorely mauled on the back hill, crushed to bits by a cow protecting its calf. I was too young to remember the details, but folk said he should have known better. I imagine him lying in the long grass with his ribs stoved in like a smashed accordion and grand clouds rolling by without a shrug. Arms and legs were broken as a matter of course, and cattle were 'man's work', a gritty, fearsome struggle beneath low, grey skies. It was the perfect job if you'd been scorched by burning aviation fuel and had the strength of five men. Gathering pens were sealed with granite posts and reinforced with railway sleepers – if you came across old pens without explanation you could assume they were built to contain dinosaurs.

It's easier for everyone when cattle are kept tame and close at hand. There's nothing inherently wild or dangerous about Galloways, and the beasts are mainly gentle in their way. They're slaves to their greed, and those heavy, snub-nosed heads can be bound in halters with a little coaxing. Any cow can kill you, and it seems unfair that Galloways should have a bad name.

My work with conservation and curlews had led me back in the direction of farming, but the tipping point came when I walked with my wife around the agricultural show at Castle

Douglas and saw the old show lines again. My grandfather had been dead for twenty years and his herd was long dispersed, but here was a line of black cattle standing shoulder to shoulder beneath a rough, burning sun as if they'd not moved an inch in all that time. Perhaps there were not as many of them as there had been, but the animals were utterly permanent. The tannoy returned and I looked up from the bustling show to see fifteen miles of blue hill country towards Carsphairn and Dalry as if it had just sat up in bed. The bold, steady cows had rolled down from that land as surely as rain after a wet night; the purest distillation of place was conveyed in flowing black hair and foamy lips. My knees almost buckled beneath me. Here at last was a true point of entry to my own place. I turned to my wife and whispered, 'We're going to have cattle.' To her eternal credit, she nodded.

Many young people find it hard to get started in farming. The industry looks like a closed shop to outsiders, but my family gave me a foothold as I began to focus on agriculture again. Rather than forge a new road from scratch, I just had to clear some brambles and cobwebs from an existing path. I asked our tenant for advice on getting started and he suggested that I take two of our fields back in hand, the rougher, less productive areas where I could find space for a few calves. The way was strangely clear, and the memory of those black animals at the show fell to a constant, nagging pulse in the back of my brain.

I took a step towards farming and found an old, familiar friend. I could slip in beneath heavy, hairy skins and find a whole new world. After thirty years in Galloway, I was finally heading home.

GRANITE

January

Low cloud and heavy rain.

Wild geese pass over the house in the morning and land in the fields by the river. The water grows fat and sluggish, then it spills its guts onto the grass. The world is reduced to a series of blue silhouettes, and still more rain lashes against the skylight and makes the glass crackle like newspaper.

No good will come of this day, but the cows need hay and the work cannot be postponed. Light, flossy bales come down from the hayshed rafters where mice cheep and scuttle. The bundles smell of sweet summer, but those fond memories are soon quashed and slushy in the mud. The twine is slit and the bales burst into flakes and sodden beasts make mirk with their heavy breath.

Galloways have a long, curly, double coat which can turn away the rain. I watch the water running off their backs and down their sides like a straw raincoat. Their only concession to this weather is to stand with their arses into the wind. They form a corral and the weather breaks upon them as if they were rocks on the shore. Once they have finished feeding, they will return to the shelter of peat haggs, whin bushes or granite scree. These animals are more comfortable outdoors on rough ground than they would be in a shed.

For all the darkness, now is a moment for snowdrops; the first skylark sings in a glimmer of light. These are fine details which might be overlooked in the busy clamour of June or July, but now they are a klaxon and a call to arms after months of starlit darkness; there is life in the world. Going about my work in these brief days, I stack snapshots in passing which combine to make the heart swell – the change is warm and strong.

I see:

The first shelduck on the wet fields, his raucous red bill reflected in a low sun
Toads on the roads, hundreds marching darkly under black and dribbling clouds
Hares running in the frost before dawn, a frizz of excitement from sober old hands.

Two sunlit days stand back to back in a flood of cold rain, and I am dazzled by their frozen mornings. A jumble of mallard cackles as they loop over the bog alders and pass round to the loch. Now is the time for their enthusiasm to spill over; drakes fight in flight for supremacy. Frogs creak in a backwater where teal have roosted the day before; the slimy creeps are couched to their eyes in a foaming soup of sex and spawn.

Snowdrops again, and now four skylarks above the moss. Herds of curlews are breaking up and growing restless for the high hills and the promise of breeding. There is a clean smell of cattle under a cloudless sky. We have two days to feel a vibration of spring, then a tumbling curtain of sleet sets the clock back to winter again.

The Celts used to celebrate this time. They called it *imbolc*: the first quiet steps out of winter. The word means something like ‘swelling’, and the festival comes when the cows begin to show their udders. Those folk were obsessed with cattle, and it made sense to celebrate the promise of new growth. I was hooked on *imbolc* when I found it because I was longing for my first calves and could almost feel the ancient excitement of new teats. The Christians tried to undo many of the old festivals, but *imbolc* left a stubborn mark. In the end, they absorbed the festival and called it Candlemas. I am no spiritualist and I did not mean to mess with pagan gods, but they began to mess with me. There are many ways to make sense of Galloway.

*

After three years by the sea, my wife and I had the chance to move. A farmhouse came up for sale, and some land was offered with it. It was close enough to visit while our supper was in the oven.

The place is visible from the main road, but I’d passed it for thirty years without ever seeing it. Farms like these don’t attract attention. You look through them and see nothing more than a splash of whitewash in a sea of stone, moss and blue, rounded fells.

The farm had belonged to an old boy who lived his entire life here and died at the age of ninety-two. I didn’t know Wullie Carson; I seem to be the only person in Galloway who didn’t. Everybody liked old Wullie, but he saw his retirement coming and lacked a younger man to take the reins. A cold spring killed his love for lambing, so he sold off all but a sliver of his farm to a neighbour and spent the last few years of his life in peace.

We fell in love with the place, but it took nine months for us to save and negotiate the financial arrangements. It was a big step up the property ladder, if you believe in things like that, and those bleak days of desperate longing seemed to pass in slow torment. In the end it was Wullie himself who tipped the balance in our favour. The old boy hadn't had electric lights until the nineties and pumped his water from the well by hand. Places like these are usually snapped by property developers who convert them into holiday cottages and stable blocks, then flip them back onto the market for the delectation of wealthy buyers from south of the border. But we heard that prospective developers had been sorely turned off by the old-fashioned style and layout of the farm. It was too much work, and that gave us time to get our ducks in a row.

We stretched every penny we had and begged for some we didn't. We talked of all the plans we had for that place, and we were suddenly glad that our family hadn't begun on schedule. We'd never have contemplated that leap with a baby in tow. Children had brought a weight of responsibility to our friends, and that killed off any discussion of risk. Even our wildest pals had been cowed by parenthood, and their smouldering ambitions were pressed into quiet caution. So it was easy to be glad of our delay on the day we collected the keys to our farm and ran, holding hands, through the close and into our new fields. This land would be our core for the cattle to come, linked to land we'd borrow from my parents and others. If we lived in the Highlands, you'd call it a big croft, a scattering of paddocks and fields across two parishes. Suddenly we had a place to get started.

I described our fields to farming friends and they asked if it was poor land. The question might have been an impudence in Angus or Berwickshire, where poverty is a shameful thing, but we'd all lived with poor land for too long to be coy; here it's a pragmatic question. We reply that it is poor in the knowledge that roughness and difficulty is a fact of life in these parts and folk will nod and shrug with resigned sympathy.

Galloway is a jumble of geology. Rolling waves of sediment and crumbly whinstone are spattered with gouts of coarse granite. Our place lies on a blister of that volcanic stone, and the nearby town of Dalbeattie is famous for it. They say that Dalbeattie granite is the best in the world, and they used to quarry it from the hills above the town. Huge blocks were ripped up by the roots and the stone was shipped away to be made into lighthouses and harbours from Sri Lanka to Trinidad. Pathé News filmed 'the Granite Men of Dalbeattie' blasting the cliffs and carting stone to be shaped and cut in the 1920s. There's a good shot of twenty men standing on a cart full of high explosives. They're all smoking cigarettes as if being blown up by a stray spark was just part of a day's work.

There's no tougher stone than Dalbeattie granite. That's a fact, but builders buy on price these days. You can get cheaper materials from China and Brazil, and so the quarry was closed and the Granite Men were sent away. Modern engineers are staggered by the work those men did by hand and horse. You'd need grand machines and hydraulic rams to do it now, and I begin to wonder if the Granite Men were really giants or titans who made the world and then vanished. Their work lives on in thunder; the hollow shell of their old quarry is enough to make you gape. We walk in their wake like weakling kids.

Further out from the town, the fields are scored and mapped with stacks of grey stone. Dykes snake and puzzle around the farms in a thousand tiny angles, then course away into the hills in striding leaps. Dalbeattie dykes bear no relation to the tidy bookstack walls you find in other places.

Our dykes are something else. You need a ton of unshaped granite to build a six-foot length. Each boulder has to be hefted up and twisted into position by hand, then pinned with smaller fragments of granite so the whole thing locks together. Forget chipping or shaping this stuff to fit; that's a non-starter. Pile three spherical boulders on top of one another and the stack is head high; it's your job to make it stay put. They used to test the quality of these dykes by getting a man to walk along the top pushing a wheelbarrow full of stone. You can still do it on some dykes which have been standing for two centuries.

Our dykes are a work of art, and they blur so beautifully into the landscape that it sometimes feels like they were always here. The truth is that almost all of them were thrown up in the first few years of the eighteenth century. Galloway was a down-at-heel place in those days, but the Union of Scotland and England gave us a shot in the arm. We were well placed to exploit John Bull's endless hunger for beef, and local landowners raised up new herds of cattle. They started to build dykes and turned the old common grazings into modern fields. This was our first real step towards agricultural 'improvement', but many poorer folk were forced off the land to make room for the cattle.

Of course there was a backlash. The people of Galloway hated those cattle, which seemed to stand for little more than selfish greed. Gangs of rioters gathered in the gloaming to pull down the new dykes with ropes and long poles. The rebels were known as 'Levellers' and were led by Billy Marshall, the man who called himself King of the Randies and the Caird of Barullion. They killed the cows with pikes and daggers, and things got so bad that government dragoons were called in to break them up. It was power and money that crushed the Levellers in the end, and it wasn't long before the dykes were rebuilt and the fields restocked. Fifty years after the revolt, maps of Scotland were published which described Galloway as 'a wild and continuous heath, feeding vast herds of cattle'. You might look at the dykes and the cattle nowadays and say that nothing is more like Galloway, but the coming of this old world spelled the death of an even older one. People say Billy Marshall died at the age of 120 and left a thousand wild tales in his wake. They don't make them like that any more.

My first days on our ground were swallowed up with restoration and maintenance. Our thin fields were laid out by dykes, but many had fallen. Even the best stretches were patched with wire and broken pallets, and they called out for resurrection. So I mended the dykes and carried that responsibility for a few years. It's a heavy job, and at first I lacked the knack to do it well. Sometimes my work fell back into the moss, but there were days when I could stand off and fail to see which sections were mine. My stones stood seamless beside others which have been in place for a century, overlapping with folk who have come and gone. I worked in silence and wondered if these stones were ever pulled down by the Levellers. There's no such thing as a clean slate in Galloway, and I can only take my lead from what I know.

The granite is sharp and cold. It bites through my leather gloves and wipes my fingerprints away into purple welts. Maybe I've already begun to lose something of myself in this work. Some of the stones make my shoulders pop in their sockets, and my body frets that dyking will become a habit; I grow a layer of callus to give extra protection in future. All this horn will do is add an extra click to the tip tap of computer keyboards, and for now the work is just pain. I'll need to toughen up if I'm going to make it here, and I'm pathetically grateful when dusk falls and I can slink back to the warm house through a rising gale of sleet and flying ice.

*

The time came to think of buying cattle. I began to ask around, but it was inevitable that I should be drawn to those black beasts which had haunted my childhood. I made a beeline to the Galloway Cattle Society for advice on getting started.

That Society has a wealth of members across the world. The breed has been sidelined by progress and change in the last half-century, but many folk are still united by their love of good beef and handsome cattle. I went to one of their meetings and was knocked flat by the depth of devotion and knowledge in that small room. It was humbling to realise that I had no idea what I was doing. Somebody asked me why I wanted to invest in Galloway cattle, and I struggled to provide an answer that wasn't lightweight or sentimental. We haven't measured our wealth in cattle for centuries, but the keeping of cows is not a game. Think long and hard, young man. My wife laughed that I was ready for the bind of parenthood but baulked at the cold reality of buying cattle. In my defence, I'd never been asked to explain why I wanted a child.

I stood back and looked again at what I wanted. There's a slim financial case for cattle in conservation. Some people make it work because they play the grants and apply for the right subsidies, but curlews don't pay the bills off their own back. Our beasts would have to do much more than drift around and help the birds. It was easy to get tangled up with fine details of conservation and wildlife, forgetting that everything depends on finance and a stable business.

I was brought up in a house which adored meat. Even in thinner days when my father straddled work with a law degree, we'd still enjoy cuts of beef that would shame the finest city restaurants. Our meat came to us from family and friends in sheets of rustling brown paper, straight from the butcher's bench. My mother worked these bundles into hot, bleeding slabs of pink flesh, oozing gravy and fine scents. We were like drug dealers guzzling our own stash, and the bones would boil into stock for soup. Perhaps I picked it up from my father, but I still believe that the finest meal in the world lies between two pieces of bread: cold roast beef in a half-inch slice, decked in butter and a sprinkle of salt.

I burned with pride to hear Galloway beef being celebrated across the world, and I was tickled by the thought that I could produce food to match the finest of its kind. Maybe I couldn't make conservation pay the bills, but there was clearly cash to be found in fine farm produce. I began to build a stronger case for farming and discovered a growing demand for traditional meat from rare breeds. Canny farmers add value to their produce because punters want to buy a piece of their heritage, a product which speaks loudly and goes beyond the daily shuttle of pink mince and vacuum packs.

I circled back to cattle with something like a credible plan. I could start with a few heifer calves and grow them into breeding stock, selling the best and eating the rest. This kind of farming is absurdly slow. Six or seven years would pass before I would have any animals to kill, and there was time to hone the specific details of my business plan on the hoof. And there was plenty of scope to throw in the towel and pass them on if it wasn't working.

*

Brisk progress followed the first enclosures and the arrival of commercial cattle in Galloway. Forward-thinking farmers tuned in to the idea of improvement because there was decent money to be made. Cattle breeding became a local obsession, and Galloway farmers seemed to have a knack for it. In 1798 an anonymous English writer praised us for creating a beast which was not being 'improved by the use of bulls from other quarters but by the unremitting efforts of breeders to use the best and most handsome cattle of both sexes, and by good feeding and management'. The genetic purity of Galloway livestock has been worn as a badge of honour ever since.

Beef was gathering steam. Look up the old records and you find a surge in cows across Galloway in the late eighteenth century. Our parish is called Kirkgunzeon (kirGUNyon), and it rose out of poverty like a comet as cattle caught on. A snapshot in 1790 described a wild and rugged land with 2,000 beasts living on it. Less than fifty years later we had over 3,000 cattle and every effort strived for more. Cash helped to focus the mind, and the English market was inexhaustable. Londoners raved about our beef, and demand grew in Manchester, Liverpool and Birmingham. In the days when hides and tallow made good prices, we were turning out the most valuable cattle in Britain, often by more than two pounds a head over other breeds.

Progress flowed on the back of our beef. By 1844 the Rev. John Crocket, minister of the parish, was proud to say that farmhouses in Kirgunzeon 'which were formerly in a miserable state, are now comfortable and commodious', with slate roofs and well-appointed yards. It was him and holy men like him who basked in the divinity of this progress. Galloway was making ground in the age-old battle against sin and wastefulness. They reckon that 30,000 head of cattle were crossing the border into England every year, and by 1800 Scottish drovers walked the cattle down to East Anglia so they could be fattened on English turnips and killed at Smithfield Market. That journey took the bellowing herds down through the heart of England, and the animals were a walking advertisement for the skill of Galloway farmers.

The original herds of Galloway cattle probably looked like a muddle, a churning mix of black, red, brown (dun) and white animals. Some were 'belted' with a white band around their bellies, and there were all kinds of other markings and patterns which lay somewhere in between. As momentum gathered, farmers began to focus on pure black cattle – 'black, black and only black' as the saying goes. The Galloway Cattle Society was established in 1878 and set down many of the conventions which had become habit. They decreed that only three colours should be recognised as true. Red and dun were popular, but black was king. Black Galloways would go on to power the beef industry in the south of Scotland for the next century, and in time they'd cast a broad shadow across the world.

The future was less promising for animals which failed to conform. Some of the oldest Galloways were black animals with a white stripe along their spines and under their bellies. These were called 'riggit' Galloways, pointing to the pitched white 'rigg' on their back. Irish farmers made a fetish of these same beautiful markings, and they developed the beautiful Droimeann and Moiled breeds with the same white line. Maybe that's where our riggs came from to start with, but whatever the explanation, riggit markings were not approved by the Galloway Cattle Society. The beasts were held to be scruffy and obscure. We wanted nothing more to do with them.

The genes which govern riggit markings are recessive and the pattern is easily suppressed. By contrast, black Galloway genetics are absurdly dominant; put a black Galloway with any other breed and the calf will be always be black and hornless. Even a red, horny Highlander will toe the line. Nature seemed to be steering farmers towards conformity, and riggit calves were no longer kept for breeding. The Society built a structure which allowed farmers to focus and refine their efforts, but it also ironed out rich seams of variety. A fine, subtle shred of our ancient agricultural heritage was rushed out of sight in a few short years.

Riggits continued to pop up here and there over the next century in a series of bizarre genetic throwbacks. Humans soon forgot them, and unexpected riggit calves were seen as inexplicable freaks. My grandfather worked with Galloway cattle all his life, but he'd have been stumped by the sight of a riggit. In contrast, his grandfather would have recognised riggits immediately and maybe would've thought that judging a cow by its markings was a fairly shallow business.

It happened that a beautifully marked riggit calf was born in the 1980s near Kirkcudbright. Like many others before her, the little heifer came as a bolt from the blue. Both of her parents had been pedigree Galloways, and there was nothing to suggest that a riggit calf could even be possible from the pairing. The farmer was puzzled, but he raised the calf and set her on the road to being a fine young beast. Whatever the explanation for those bizarre markings, the heifer had no value as a breeding animal. It's no use worrying about these things, and at least she'd make a good carcass at the abattoir in Castle Douglas.

The tale turns strange when you hear that another riggit calf was born that year on a different farm a few miles away. Here was a little bull, just as unexpected. Throwbacks like these happen now and again, but two at once in the same place is something extraordinary. There was no reason for either farmer to do any more than shrug, but they were curious enough to find out more. A crucial piece of evidence lay in a painting by the Regency artist George Garrard. Captioned 'A Fat Galloway Heifer at Smithfield Christmas Show – 1804', the painting clearly shows a riggit Galloway with a white head, a white rigg and classic markings from tail to snout. The weird, throwback calves suddenly had a name and a heritage; they were every bit as pure and authentic as the finest pedigree stock. It was obvious that they should be paired.

With the backing of friends in high places, riggit Galloways began a long climb out of obscurity. Some people actively disliked the riggits and thought they were mongrels which gave the pure Galloway a bad name. A few took active steps to stymie the riggit's resurrection, but other farmers were persuaded to keep their own throwbacks and use them for breeding. The markings were quietly kindled back into life, but always in tiny numbers and often clustered around southern England. Now there's even a Riggit Galloway Cattle Society, which serves as a network for people who love the markings. The animals are registered 'pedigree', as much as that's possible.

Some people still say that riggit Galloways are worth nothing at all because you can't breed them true. That's a fair point. Put a riggit bull with a riggit cow and you still need to roll the dice for a riggit calf. You might end up with something that's black or white or somewhere between, but that's how the old herds used to work. The important thing is that these are Galloway cattle and they're defined by unpredictable markings. There's no such thing as the 'perfect riggit', and in a world of cast-iron regulations, that creates some nice space for personal preference.

A handful of riggit Galloways remain in Galloway, and I went to see my first beasts as an act of curiosity on a warm, sunlit evening in September. Restless swallows crowded along the telephone wires which connect Balmaclellan to the outside world, and the moor smelled of old bracken and dry moss. We climbed up through light fields until the land opened up beyond us. Hills loomed over a winding loch, the drab, familiar shapes of Corserine, Cairnsmore and the Garroch.

The cows belonged to Richard, and he is good with his animals. He's gentle and softly spoken, and he chatted to them as if they were dear old friends. He checked off their details on a folded piece of paper, then he clasped his hands quietly behind his back. Some heifer calves were for sale, and we could have stood barefoot in the soft grass as they walked between us. Of course I was smitten. These beasts smelled of cud and honesty, lightly shaken from the leaves of a history book. I drank them in and found that they were home incarnate; a place conjured up in curls and long, soft eyelashes.

I warmed to the riggit colours in a heartbeat; blacks and whites swirled together like a freshly poured pint of stout. I'd always been dead set on black Galloways, but there was no way I could ever walk away from these animals. I chose one calf for her markings, which were a perfect replica of the old Garrard painting of 1804. She was blotchy, soft and perfectly gorgeous. I picked a second for her shape – a broad, tubby barrel with a wrinkle of fat around her neck. Richard shook my hand and we sealed the deal, but there was a squeak of dishonesty on my part. I didn't have any money to pay for these calves, but I reassured myself that there were still three months to worry about that. The heifers were young and couldn't leave their mothers until Christmas, giving me enough time to scrape some cash together. Three months keened my appetite to a fever pitch. Having reconsidered his options over the autumn, Richard telephoned again and offered me two more beasts. I went to the bank.

It turned out that my first heifers were absurdly independent. I was ready to care for them, but they didn't need anything from me. They came out of the lorry, vanished into the whins, and I didn't see them again for a week. I fell to tracking their movements like a big game hunter. That makes them sound nervy and wild, but really it was a knowing adolescent coolness which kept them at arm's length. I'd been told that they would be 'low maintenance' but found that they were 'no maintenance'. They made it clear that my duty was to feed them and then get lost.

One of my calves was the most beautiful animal I'd ever seen. She had a white head with black eyes, black ears and a black nose. We call these markings 'points', and here's the seed of beauty. 'Well-marked' cattle start with deep, expressive eyes which glitter in dribbled mascara. Beyond this, riggit markings can be almost anything. The main requisite is a white stripe which runs from the withers to the rump, but my favourite was mottled all over. Her sister had a black head and a white arse. The third was dappled with blue roan and the fourth was daubed with blocky, geometrically perfect markings with hard lines. They were a jumble and I adored their details, but I couldn't ignore the fact that these animals aren't supposed to be viewed up close. Pat and dandle them all you like, but Galloways look best in a middle distance of tumbling moorland and rising cloud. At the range of a mile, riggits make a smattered line of black and white to make your heart sing. It is possible to breed red riggit Galloways, and the colour is popular with English breeders. I was struck with black riggits because they're bound to the same spartan aesthetic as granite and collie dogs; even our house is white with black lintels. This landscape swings in a million shades, but black and white is utterly permanent.

Six months passed before I'd even touch my calves. Bound up and confined in a steel crush, the vet drew blood samples for a health check. The needles bent at the hardness of their skin and the blood flowed dark and thick into a plastic tube. I waited until the vet was looking away, then reached in shyly to touch my beasts. They were warm and rough and their hair was filled with whin prickles. A smell of sweat and cud tingled on my palm. Even at hip-height, they were bigger than toys and could tread me into the mud without a shrug.

It's often hard to draw a line between Galloways and Galloway itself. The cattle were formed by that rough, grassy land which runs across the Southern Uplands like sack cloth, and yet the moors themselves are a product of their grazing. These hills were an ancient forest in the days before men came and began to reorganise the place. So it's fair to reckon that the moors and the animals are really just the same thing. And if you're happy with that, then it's not such a big leap to imagine that the beef is really just a fine concentration of that damp, empty void between low clouds and the peat moss.

The bond between hills and beasts feels ancient, but there's something horribly fragile in that link between cattle and moorland places. The world began to move away from Galloway cattle over the last half-century, and many of the old herds have now vanished. It should be no surprise that cow-made places have begun to misfire and underperform as cattle withdraw. Our wide hills are no longer feeling themselves, and it's starting to become clear how deeply the old connection ran between hill country and curly beasts. Galloways gave us more than just meat; they were the heart of a very old system.

I remember the pyres which followed the Foot and Mouth outbreak in 2001. The streets were filled with soldiers and vets in white overalls. A sickly smell lay in the glens, and smoke poured up from stiff-legged heaps of dead stock. If a farm tested positive for the disease, all animals within a three-kilometre radius were killed. The awful diktat raked through the landscape and brought a sudden, jarring end to many famous beasts.

Hills are no place for hurry or quick changes. Farming this land is like walking across a broad spread of open ground. You lay your plans on a distant rock, then set off towards it. The work rolls by and every step takes you irresistibly closer to the destination that you saw in its wholeness before you started. You can get away with angles and quick thinking on good ground, but the hills demand a slow and stable plod. Fertility grows, habits form and the land is teased into action. People and animals pass down their wisdom between generations. Cows had been in the hills for thousands of years; far back beyond the first farmers. The culls snapped a million ancient threads and left hill farmers with sudden decisions.

A friend in the Glenkens still mourns the loss of his cattle, which used to walk the five-mile track to and from his hill without any pushing or encouragement. The brave old cattle were driven by nothing more than a pulse of memory and routine. All he had to do was walk behind them and close the gates. They've been gone for years, but you can sometimes hear those old herds moving in the darkness. Their habits are worn into the soil like hoofprints, and calves learned the land from their mothers. Farmers were compensated for their losses, but you can't replace that weighty heft of shared memory.

Stripped of cattle, the land took a new path. Cows had been smashing up bracken and deep beds of rough grass for centuries. They kept a balance and built a blend of freshness in the undergrowth. Curlews loved that mix and thrived in the wake of old cattle. They riddled the rich mud for worms, and their chicks fattened in a fairyland of insects and spiders which hummed around the dark pats. But without the munching mouths, heather began to drown in ribbons of white grass and the wildflowers thinned to exhaustion. Curlews were baffled because the ground grew thick and dull beneath them. The cattle had sustained a fine, subtle footing in a fragile world, but they were burnt and buried and everything changed.

We can never measure the loss of old hill cows. We're only just beginning to see that our trusty old natives called for a kind of farming which improved everything it touched. And now our wildlife is hamstrung without them; the crashing decline of birds like curlews is just a symptom of our withdrawal from tough, tricky places. Now it's easier to make the hills into something new, and policy-makers are nudging farmers to ditch their livestock and sow their hills with commercial forests. This is the final straw for curlews. The birds have lived beneath open skies for too long to tolerate trees. They abandon the hills where plantings grow, and the survivors fail and rot beneath strange new pressures from the trees.

Change usually comes in a long, nibbling flow of details. We look up one day and realise that we've been travelling all the while. It's harder to fathom change in Galloway because it came in a single, unchewed lump. We moved from ancient, primordial woodland to farming over a thousand years. We turned our hand to cattle over several centuries. Then we became a commercial softwood forest in thirty years.

And people say nothing happens in Galloway.

HILLS

February

Snow has trapped us in this house for days, just two of us. It's a joy. We curl around one another like bears in a den, but I mourn the slight progress we had made towards spring. The birds have gone, and this might as well be midwinter again.

A neighbour came to visit with bread and milk in a tractor. We thanked him, but we had supplies to last and didn't need much. He stamped his boots on the mat and passed on shreds of gossip. I thought the world had ended with snow, but we learned that Castle Douglas is busy and green – it's business as normal just a few miles away. Our apocalypse is an exception.

We heard that the gateways are scored with drifts, and sheep lie dead in their dozens at the dyke backs. Horn tips will begin to poke above the melting snow in a month – markers which show the ravens where to dig. It's as bad as anyone can remember, but for now there is silence and spindrift stirs a hissing burr like caster sugar upon itself. Lights flicker, and we are put back in our box.

I left the cattle when the snow was flying. They don't need me to keep them warm, but I lay in bed and listened to the dreary smirr as it rushed over the hill. If I stumbled out to check on them, they'd stand and stretch and lose their cosy fug. Far better to leave them lying, but it's a leap of faith. I have to trust them.

And now it's morning. Sunlight and blue frost has baked a crust onto the snow. I watch a hare preening his breast as the kettle boils, and later I find the cattle lying in a loose gang on the hill. Their steam rises up into clear, blaring skies. They walk to me and I dump their bales on a ledge of granite so that they have something hard to stand on. Then I step back to the wooden gate and watch them dine in a cloud of breath which swirls around them in the stillness like dry ice. They jostle and toss their heads, and then a bitter breeze comes to ripple the long hair on their backs. Beyond them lies thirty miles of southern Scotland, a rolling sea of slush and rough grass with the sun trailing rags of light across the middle distance. The place seems wholly empty, and I can understand the shrugging blankness of friends who come here and see nothing at all. They rarely rock on their heels and sigh in wonder. You don't always see it at first.

I am ready to leave them when my eye is drawn to the dark atom of a distant fox. He is trotting his way along the top of the dyke like a bird, bouncing his toes on the rough stones. It occurs to me that he is on that dyke because he doesn't want to get his feet wet. Such catty little dogs. They don't like this weather, and I try to imagine his quiet disgust at a heavy fall of snow. This is tough country for foxes; there is more than weather against them.

He winds along the tops and only sees me when he is quite close. He freezes. Cold light makes him seem dull and dark, but I know every jammy note in that pelt. There is purple and grey, marmalade and smoke in his mane. He looks to the cattle as if they should have warned him I was here, then drops quietly away into the thickness of deep grass. Wet feet after all.

Ten days after leaving school, I was being trained as a gamekeeper by a man who had killed thousands of foxes in his life. He often said what a grim day it would be if we ever caught the last one. I have killed hundreds, but never without a swell of regret.

The cows are a tangle of black and white, and a raven flies above them. My knuckles have passed beyond the pain of cold, and I realise there will be more pain before they are warm again. A jet streaks against the high blue sky, streaming a chalky white line behind it. It is heading for Newfoundland, and the sound arrives like a curling stone on ice.

*

The new forests grew well in Galloway. Most of the trees came from Alaska and Canada, and the foresters were delighted to find that they grow better here than they do in the New World. Our old hills were split into blocks, and tractors pulled heavy ploughs through the whispering grass. Men followed the black scars with bags of sapling trees, and they plugged the furrows with miles of stems and needles. The world was utterly remade.

Thirty years later, the broad moors have been marshalled into dark and draughty crops which run for miles in every direction. Follow tracks into those new forests and you walk in the slot of a black gutter. Now and then you'll find a ride which intersects your tangent. You get a chance to gaze along it, and maybe there'll be some fragment of horizon at the end. But take a step forward or back and you'll lose it again.

You can forget the idea of striking out to explore the new plantations. You wouldn't make it twenty feet off the path. The twigs are dry and they saw your skin like a rank of knives; you give up because you've come here to enjoy yourself and there's no fun in that half-bent misery as the needles rain down your collar and make your skin raw.

They've built monuments to the men who did this planting work, and they celebrate the labour which conjured progress out of waste. There's no doubt that planting was an epic feat, but new worlds have a habit of crushing their forebears. Foresters say that nothing good happened until the trees came; we should be glad that there's money to be made at last.

We've paid a sore price for this progress, but we can't measure the cost and form a true balance. Lots of people work in the sawmill, but now the rivers are sour and the fish are killed by poisons from the forests. Timber makes valuable chipboard and wood pulp, but our ancient peatlands have been razed by ploughs and they dribble away like mud. We've lost our mountain hares, our black grouse and our eagles as the forests grew. Golden plovers are no more, and now salmon fade into silence. Years pass and the trees become easier to stomach because we can't remember a time before them.

In the days before I was born, Galloway was a tapestry of rough farms, hill cattle and open moorland which ran in an unbroken sweep for seventy miles between Stranraer and Dumfries. The land had lain in this groove for so long that it seemed to have no beginning. We forgot about the Levellers and riggit Galloways because our progress had fallen to a limpid, curdling crawl. We thought that change was just a thing for weathervanes, and it's no wonder we were stunned by the coming of new forests.

I arrived in the 1980s, when the moors were mumbling to the tune of ploughs and planters. I never saw this place before the trees, and there's no reason for me to mourn the loss of old Galloway. I only know that place through stories and old photographs, but there's a constant thread of memory which pulls me backwards.

Nostalgia is a dirty word, and I spring away from it. Nostalgic writers are slain for their trouble because we don't need nostalgia where we're going. I might just as well long for the world of Billy Marshall and his tinker folk or the ancient woods which grew from the ruins of the last Ice Age. It makes no logical sense to claw at this most recent loss, which is just the latest of many. But I'm too late to know the old world, and too early to forget it. I'm stuck in the middle and I'm scarred by the loss of wide places and lonely, calling birds.

Now the wounds are healing. There are some people who come here because they love our new forests, and I sometimes wish I could join them. Life would be easy if I could accept this place as it is now. I wouldn't miss a thing, and maybe I'd grow to love the plantations too. But I plunge away instead. I dive off the beaten track to torment myself with whispers of the old ways. Every year makes it harder to connect with the world I love. The forests have grown and near places have become far. If you fight and push through the new trees for long enough, you sometimes stumble into a clearing and find an abandoned house in the deep forest. Sometimes it's no more than a rowan tree and a pile of stones to show where people lived and ran their land. Then the black wall of trees rears up again, and your long-forgotten yard is just a shady pit in a treetop world.

Curlews have got no use for trees and they hate the new forests. Their old breeding grounds were drowned in a rising flow of dark, industrial conifers. That made them anxious, but the new plantations brought crows and foxes in heavy abundance. They dribbled out of the trees and they found good hunting on the open ground. Curlews were robbed and killed until they could stand it no longer, and soon the old hills were quiet. The death of the curlew is complex and confusing, but now we see that their hearts were broken by the forester's plough.

I've met folk who say that curlews are dead and gone – we should forget about them. Their problems now run so deep that we just can't bail them out. More than three-quarters of Galloway's hill country has been planted with trees since the Second World War. There are some parishes where it's hard to find a scrap of open land, but now there are calls for even more plantations, and politicians are being taught to think of moorland landscapes as the forests of the future. That looming step will complete our transformation. The final curlews won't endure it.

At first, I fought the foresters. I screamed against the rising tide of trees and wrote noisy articles. I bought a camera and began to take photographs of everything. I gathered up bundles of old letters and picture books of people in this place, and I stacked them in heaps beside my desk. Every flake of paper was fragile and important because the world was being smashed to bits before my eyes. It's hard to oppose the planting of new forests without looking like a nut: the trees are good for business. But there were many losers when they came to Galloway. My special interest was curlews, but the damage ran far beyond birds into human lives and habits. The landscape vanished under those plantations. The hill farms were turfed out, and our old ways swirled into the sky like dry grass.

Having been raised on a diet of ancient tales and folklore, my home was a prefilled hand-me-down. I couldn't imagine my own life without the frame and comfort of history. I wanted the same for my own children when they came, but all those foundations and guy ropes were being spooled away into the darkness. So I began to write about the people who lived on hill farms. I recorded conversations with family friends and I stashed their stories in an archive. I'd always been a keen collector, but even I found some of this stuff dry and hard to grasp: guidance on setting a good peat fire, tips for shoeing a heavy horse. You could bind those recordings together and call them a survival guide for a damn hard place, but much of the rest was laughter and reflection, with long pools of silence and the crackle of old newspaper.

I gathered all that around me with a growing sense of panic because nobody else was interested. For all we're proud of this place and the fine history we've made, we aren't good at protecting it. Time after time, I'd bump up against a weary, pragmatic fatalism, that Galloway is gone and there's no point clutching for the bones of it. We've always been a working place, and the trees are just where the market took us next.

It would be easier to let the old traditions go if we could agree on what should come next. Some of my friends see nothing special about this place. They were born here and belong to the far south-west, but they laugh to hear me insist on dividing Dumfries from Galloway as if it mattered. Young folk think Dalbeattie is a pale imitation of Glasgow and they're gagging to leave. I can imagine how they might hate it here, with no jobs and nothing to do. Kids come out and smash bottles in the park, and old folk tut and twitch their curtains, saying it was never like this in the old days.

Our neighbours in the Lake District have reinvented themselves as the leisure and recreation capital of England. The foresters came for them too, but their hills are famous and people rallied round to fend them off. Now millions go to see the fells, and long queues wait for their turn on the high ground. We're less enthusiastic about tourism, and most of our hills are crumpled and trackless. Many of us dig in our heels and curse the tourists for their nosiness. There's a legal right to roam across the entirety of Scotland, but walkers are so rare in Galloway that I can't remember the last time I saw one.

There's a website where ramblers log their trips into the Southern Uplands. This often reads more like a list of arguments between farmers and daytrippers, and I read that one walker was told to get lost by a farmer who said, 'You've got no business up here.' I worked out which farmer it was; he's a dour type, and I wouldn't take his side for any money, but I suppose he was technically correct; the visitor hadn't come for any matter of business or trade. What little tourism we have is often brought to us indirectly; tourists buy holiday homes and rent them out to other tourists. I sometimes feel like we're missing a trick, but then I remember the cost of visitors, the rasp of car parks and the nattering scrum of coach parties, and that's when I treasure my solitude.

In a moment of proactive enthusiasm, a group of activisits pushed for Galloway to be made into a national park. They circulated a petition and planned to march their demands all the way to the parliament buildings at Holyrood. The response was quietly reserved. A fair proportion of folk preferred to keep their heads down and stay out of the spotlight. We like being quiet, but as farming and fishing decline, we're not left with many options to make the landscape pay. Foresters claim to have the answers, but the pubs keep shutting and the shops are long dead. Maybe the trees have made some folk rich, but we never see them.

I'd chosen to work as a journalist, and that industry was new and guilt-free. I wasn't planting up the hills or digging black scars into the peat, and it was easy to grumble at the people who did. My writing work was safe and passive, and I looked out on this place through my office window. The hardest choice I made was whether to risk going out without a jacket at lunchtime. I asked for beauty and wild birds, but I took them on my terms.

Then I began to sink into farming and found myself outside on blue, miserable days when I didn't want to go. Agriculture really knows how to rub your nose in a place, and you learn to depend upon it. It wasn't long before the happy novelty of feeding cattle began to fade; I started to strain away from the work. So much of farming is drab repetition – the same and the same for weeks until the thought of it fairly sickens you when the alarm goes off and there's rain on the window again. I began to sulk at the morbid slog of feeding and checking stock. But it was hard to ignore jewels among the black, fogbound days. Suddenly the mist would part and I would see some hagg or ledge from an unexpected angle. And I'd gape in excitement at the inbound shade of rushing rain which swirled and churned over a mile of grass before it found me; spots of it on my face at first, then a rasping burr to bring flame into my ears.

Now and then I'd be taken by the flare of grouse or the speck of an owl hunting over the grass. Then I was glad of the blackness, which you'd never find in a diet of sunny days. And a group of vagrant curlews, which came to me at the end of our second week in a moment of blank resignation. I'd slumped for a coffee and found shelter in the lee of a tall granite dyke. Two dozen birds came rounding in to feed below me, but I could hardly see beyond the blood in my blisters and the rain down my back. I looked at them as if they were sleet or birling grass. That's when I began to make progress beyond the realm of scientific textbooks and the jargon of ecology.

*

Foresters say this is a place to grow trees, but the same sodden climate drives a swell of rich grass. Hardly a day goes by in Galloway without the lash of sweet Atlantic rain, and it sometimes seems like we're always wet. I walk through a pair of wellies every six months, and grass comes to us like a flood. Cows are the path of least resistance in Galloway, although now we're more likely to keep fast-growing European beasts from Charolais or Friesland.

We're like many places where farming has specialised. Vegetables usually come from Angus, soft fruit from Perthshire and lamb from Sutherland. We've learned to maximise outputs, but lots of farms now rise and fall on a single line of productivity. There's a flurry of activity to produce silage in the summer, but otherwise the fields are cold and empty places. Massive, booming harvests are followed by long, hollow busts. It makes a hungry place for wildlife, and it's no surprise to see bird populations in freefall. It's easy to blame the foresters and their new plantations for the loss of our old world, but farming takes a fair slice of the blame.

My grandfather's world was founded on an obsession with crop rotations. One crop followed another in a steady, dependable sequence, and the lumbering pattern would coax the land into good heart. The people who invented rotations were careful and godly, and they spent their lives working to glean goodness from nature. Farmers drew huge benefit from their system, but wildlife also took a share of the spoils because mixed farming was beautifully balanced. As one crop was cut, another was sown and a third was ripening. Nobody asked the birds to come, but the soil was fit, and feathers rode the constant flux between stubbles and meadows, moorland and ploughland. The bonanza of feed and nutrients extended across glens, parishes and entire counties.

Curlews used to be shy, moorland birds. They made their home in the hills and rarely came near human beings. When the new rotations came, the land boomed so deeply that they broke ranks and poured down to breed in lush meadows and hayfields across the lowlands. They'd never show such a flair for innovation again, but that leap into farmland binds their story to ours. You can plot their expansion on a map through the late Victorian age and the decades which followed. The new birds sounded strange to Lowland folk, but soon their songs were swallowed up and adored. Curlews can do that, and it became hard to imagine life without them.

Farmers are old in Scotland. The average age is fifty-seven, and there are many folk who can still remember the crop rotations in Galloway. People followed those patterns until new methods came in the 1970s, and the dust had not long settled when I was a boy. My neighbours had fond memories of cereal crops and turnip fields, but they were quick to explain how much easier things were now that grass is king and growth depends upon artificial fertilisers. Turnips make excellent food for cattle, though it's a slim margin for all the hassle. And anyway, the weather's unpredictable, and who can afford all that equipment for the sake of a few acres? Most folk laughed at the angles I took; some were quietly intrigued. Perhaps it was their own nostalgia, but some neighbours confessed that the old ways had worked well enough and were sorry to have left them.

I couldn't help thinking of the old rotations, which naturally kneaded the soil and brought curlews tumbling down from the clouds to glut and stuff themselves in the margins. I never saw those systems working, but they seemed to offer some chance of mending the collapse of wild birds. Besides, curlews pull their grub out of the soil; they howk for worms with their pincer bills, so it made sense to start at mud level.

We've learned to get more from the best ground over the past few decades, but we've lost the skills and manpower we need to extract value from harder places. Farming is famously poor at storing unused information, and it doesn't take long for old knowledge to vanish. Just as the old hill ways were smashed by the trees, modern agriculture has snuffed out a world of know-how. Nobody ever thought to write down any of the knowledge you need to farm the old rotations. Now it's fading away and only survives in living memory. Suddenly I was glad of my sad miscellany of archives and interviews. Dredging back through my notes, I found hints and clues to get me started along the road. This kind of knowledge doesn't like being bottled and it seemed to gasp with relief when I drew it out and began to make use of it.

The old rotations relied on momentum. It's no trouble to skim a living off a grand, lumbering mill when it's up and running, but it's a sore job to get it started when it's stopped. A bit of know-how was vital, but everything I had was rusty and still. Our land had been in grass for twenty years or more, and it was only thanks to Wullie Carson's light touch that any curlews still came to the glen. He'd known the old ways and worked within their limits, but the birds were beginning to peter out in his absence. We took on his yard, his paddocks and his birds, yet you can count our curlew pairs on the fingers of one hand. They're the final sounds in a very quiet place.

I picked a small field to begin. It lay in a broad triangle behind the house, and it seemed to represent the best of what we had. It made sense to hire some help with the work, and there are all kinds of agricultural contractors in Galloway, kitted out with a comprehensive range of shiny equipment. However, my first contacts were a disaster because our fields are too small and nobody wanted the jobs I had. Most people said they couldn't justify the work. Others said they would do it and then didn't, and that was even worse.

It was time to invest even more money or abandon the project. I was steered in the direction of a tractor which came up for sale in Dumfries. The dealer tried to wangle an inflated price, and I was green enough to go along with him. Perhaps David Brown doesn't mean much these days, but his tractors were the acme of British engineering for half a century. The machine we bought predates my birth by fifteen years, a rusty white hulk with red wheels and a bizarre, angular cab like a greenhouse. The old David Brown logo was still visible beneath a flock coating of moss – a red rose beside a white one – made in Yorkshire. I was suspicious of that pedigree: my generation isn't familiar with the idea of 'British-made'. I could believe that this machine might have been assembled in England, but the parts probably came from China because everything does.

Some people buy old machinery because it fits with an old fashioned ideal of country life. Here's nostalgia again, and there are vintage tractor clubs where old men meet to polish their machines. I certainly liked the look and feel of the old equipment, but I'd bought on price and the certain knowledge that it was my own tractor or nothing at all.

But for all I'd found one within my budget, old tractors require maintenance. A fortnight had passed before I was facing my first repair job, and others came thick and fast thereafter. It seemed like I'd picked up a millstone, and I was childishly unable to do the work myself. I was never drawn to engineering and I'd always reckoned that mechanics worked some kind of magic. I asked for help, then had to confess that I didn't understand the instructions and advice I was being given. I paid an engineer to come and fix a leaking pipe, but then another problem came, and I was broke and stuck with a dead machine.

I had nothing but time on my side, so I found a manual and then picked up a set of spanners in a car-boot sale. Some of the joints came to pieces quite easily, and I thumbed through the book and found the codes for the nuts and brackets which grew in a mucky mound on the shed floor. I had to bleed the fuel injection system, and my hands were waxy with diesel as I slackened the pipes and found the bulb you press when you want to flush the air away. Bubbles came hissing out in a froth like a fart and then clean diesel pooled onto my boots. The tractor came to life again. The pads of my fingers were black, and I grinned like a cat.

I soon knew every nook and cranny of that tractor. Even if some part broke, I could salvage pride from having known that it was going to happen. I began to forget how it feels to start every task with the certainty of completion. And I remember the afternoon when I lost all access to high-range gears. There was a grinding moan, then nothing at all. I'd made good progress, but the gearbox was far beyond me. From that day, my top speed has been limited to a gentle walking pace. When I drive out to haul trailers of hay in the summer, I'm overtaken by butterflies. I shook with fury at first, but that tractor was nudging me towards a longer, slower game.

My wife and I were happy to pour our savings into this project, but we could hardly hope to build a farm from nothing. After six months, we had four calves and a tractor on thirty borrowed acres, the barest bones of a business. As the work went on, I was helped by family and friends who lent or gave me their support. That generosity was humbling, and it was doubly valuable because it seemed to confer some feeling of endorsement. I began to wonder if there was more to this than a mad act of fancy.

Having followed my progress for some time, a retired farming friend contacted me with the offer of a plough. Given my interest in crop rotations, he reasoned that I would soon be needing one. The tool was mine for the taking, and I scheduled a trip to his farm near Kelso.

I found an arable landscape in the east; I was a fish out of water. That eastern country smelled of soil and vegetables; I couldn't even identify some of the crops. I sometimes forget how monotonous this grassland place can be when compared with other parts of Scotland. It was a joy to drive through a maze of stubbles, furrows and winter cereals, a bustling blend of colours and textures. One recently ploughed field was littered with lapwings, and I slowed down to watch pairs of hares wandering through a strip of tall, broken seedheads. Larks rose up to sing above barley stubbles, and rooks stirred to and fro in the cold wind. Wildlife has been lost in the Borders over the past forty years, but they still have sparks of life which we lack in the west.

My trailer was loaded with a two-furrow plough. I was briefed on plough anatomy, and I found shoes, shins and shares beneath a scabby crust of rust. The plough had been obsolete for forty years, but it would do the job. I took to the road again and couldn't resist gazing at my new pet in the rear-view mirror as I threaded back through high hills towards Moffat. It was hard to ignore the idea that I was bringing home some part of that mixed arable richness.

Then we waited for the weather. Ploughs can't work when the soil is thick and miserable, and more snow lay for days on the sleeping fields. Wild geese paddled in the slush and trampled down the remains of last year's grass. I worked hard to make sure that the machines would be ready when the moment came. Grinders sprayed their sparks into the rain on blue days, and my hands were stained with cakes of grease. The rain finally paused, and I kept my eye on the flooded pools by the river and watched them slowly drying. It's a sure sign of progress when those pools ooze away and the fields shrink back from their bloaty fullness. Then I waited until the granite crags blew pale and dry behind the house before I moved to act.

A jumble of swans flew at first light – heavy whoopers which made the sky sing like wind over empty bottle tops. The plough was raised up on hydraulic arms, and the rust was rubbed away with a polish until the wide mouldboards shone in a low, cold sun. I could see my face in those boards, and then the tractor shuddered away from the yard into open country.

A two-furrow plough makes slow progress. Each steady pass gnaws at the turf like a planer, shaving the inches away in long, heavy curls. Bare folds of soil flopped upside down, and the shining mouldboards polished them in passing with a glossy sheen. Soon there was a long black corrugation stretching slowly out behind me, a dark scar in a cold world of green and yellow. A wagtail came to watch.

It was hard to say what the iron teeth would find beneath the grass, and I was clenched for impact. Of course there were boulders of every shape and size, but the smaller ones were rummled out into the daylight and they lay on the furrows like rubbish. The bigger ones brought the tractor to a juddering halt, and I lived in fear of breaking the plough. I tempted fate by going deep because it felt good to bring up red streaks of boiling subsoil. The earth was soon powdering in the fresh easterly breeze, and the first wagtail had become many. Little birds plundered the ground, bobbing and hunting through the troughs of soil and filling their bellies with orange grubs. Gulls bawled into the cab and I wallowed all the while in the hum of that three-cylinder diesel engine.

The tractor's noise deafened me and the roar became a new level of silence as I sat in the tall, glass cab like an ornament in a display case. This is the sound of my ploughing and my father's too, but newer tractors have insulated cabs and the drivers listen to the radio. Casting my mind back, I tried to imagine how ploughing might have sounded to my great-grandparents. Quiet, I suppose – the heavy plod of horses' hooves would have left space for the purr of ripping turf. The same task has been utterly transformed by a few short years.

I returned to walk the field beneath the moon. The smell of drink was upon me, and my ears rang with the pub's clatter. I was thinking big and pompous things that would never survive a nudge of daylight, and a curlew was moving somewhere in the stillness. I heard the lonely whistle over the moss and imagined the bird pondering her next move, back to the hills and the high ground soon.

My farming and conservation drifted easily together in slack water throughout the dark days. Winter is slow, and the cattle let the coldness pour over them like a tide. Finches glittered in the mud they made, but those little birds were nothing to write home about. It all seemed a far cry from progress and the stirring thrill of conservation, but curlews were coming home and the birds would soon begin to compete for my attention. I'd have to strike an old and careful balance.

WHAUP

March

There's a moment of gentle peace before the cattle begin to moan. Stars fade in the dawn, and I heft a pair of hay bales on my back. The twine used to hurt my fingers, but now I have ruts of callus in the groove between my pads and knuckles. It doesn't bother me anymore. I pause in a gap between two buildings at the back of the yard and watch the darkness dozing through it. I see crags and boulders in the half-light, and the horizon slumped in dullness. The day hangs in undecided silence.

Then they see me and things begin. Beasts shove and scrum, and their shit batters the frost. There's no going back now, so I loosen the gate and curse them for their barging when the latch raps me on the knuckles. I already have a black nail from this kind of carry-on, and now shreds of summer grass trickle down my neck. I call them bastards and forget to drink in their warm, belching fug which usually makes me smile.

Then I leave the cattle and head for the hills, finding friends on the high ground. The hill is burning by noon, and our fire hunts through the heather like a beast. We watch the flames crackle in a mix of blaeberry and fallen grass, and the smoke streams away from us across miles of open country towards Dumfries. There is a bitter wind, but it comes clean and stirs a wake through the writhing blaze. Grouse arrive to natter and buck in the ashes, and the chancy cocks saunter through the soot with their seedy beaks ajar. This is their moment in the sun, a time to impress the hens and stake a claim on new territories for the coming year. They nod their wattles and fight like knights in the wreckage of our fire.

I lean on the shaft of my flogger and watch flames licking through the cover. Chunks of granite emerge fresh and glittery as if the smoke were bubbles of soap. This job cleans out the old growth and sows freshness; it's one of many old ways to keep the hill moving. Some of us are driven to this task by a desire to shoot grouse in the autumn, others to improve the grazing for sheep. Some of us burn because we always have.

There was a time when every hill was burnt in Galloway, but the work is hard and it can be dangerous. We once had a fire that got away from us and ran for miles over the hill. We thrashed the embers until our palms bled, but there was no catching it again. We followed it all night, and I still rake up memories of smoke and flame in the small hours as the blaze drove deer off the hill like a collie dog. I was lifted off by a helicopter in the end, and we flew home across 1,000 acres of ash. It was a disaster, but in two years the hill had bounced back to a new level of prosperity. The lambs wobbled with fat and the grouse came back tenfold.

Folk are not keen on burning these days. Most people have stopped, and it's hard to get started again. On a clear, dry afternoon in March you might see the odd fire in the west. The plumes of smoke are few and far between, and we can always tell who is beneath them. 'That'll be Jimmy McCowan burning at the Slakes,' or 'Norrie's done well to get that lit on the back of Trostan.' I feel their eyes upon us too. We are the last of a network of beacons in the dusk.

This is a clean day to burn, and my work is small. I nudge and guide the flames into extinction. Heaps of grouse shit smoulder like incense once the fire has passed. The smoke has a sappy tang which smells like spring, and we stop in the late afternoon when the dew begins to fall and the fire growls into the doldrums. I sit on the black ground and peer through my binoculars, trying to make out my cattle. They must be lying up in some hollow, and I follow the contour for a mile to the shore where the tide is out and geese are clattering inland above the farms of friends and neighbours.

It's dark by the time I am home. I reek of heather smoke and the hair has been scorched from the backs of my hands. I smell like a ham under the stars. The cattle blink idly in my headlights.

*

Thousands of curlews come to Galloway in the winter. They churn like smoke above the horizon, and they build the illusion that all is well. Sometimes there are hundreds of birds on the flooding fields below the house, and people are reassured to hear them calling over creeks and the glugging merse. You'd never think there was a problem with curlews, but the truth is that winter birds are just visitors passing through. When the time comes to lay their eggs, those curlews will travel on to Finland or Russia. Our own come up from Brittany, and they'll often land in the same fields where they were hatched. Our problem is that fewer come back every year.

I remember the first curlew I saw in our new place. We had no guarantee that birds would return to breed here, and so many have been lost that it seemed unlikely. There was no mention of curlews in the estate agent's inventory, but the land was rough and wet and the signs were good. One morning towards the end of March, I stepped out under the stars in my dressing gown and there was a bird in the darkness. The old breeding song drooled over the moor like warm steam, and I had to steady myself on a wall.

Curlews play a long game. They come at life with the assumption of longevity, and they live to make old bones. We've got hard proof that curlews can live for thirty years and more, but scientific evidence really just confirms something we've known for centuries. Curlews were born for old age, and every creaking inch of feather and tendon finds quiet joy in antiquity.

Rather than fire out dozens of youngsters during a brief window of life, the birds pick their moments and mature slowly over several years. They're cagey and patient, and they know that there will always be another chance to get it right. While other birds dash into boom or bust, a curlew can afford to stand back and watch. In a cold spring or a dry May, they just go back to the coast. There's always next year.

At first I groped towards the idea that curlews came to Wullie Carson, but that was just whimsy. Then I learned that curlews live for decades and they're drawn to old farmers and rough country. That's when I realised the truth, and there's nothing metaphorical about it: Wullie's birds had become ours, and they'll keep coming here until they die (or I die first). I suppose I'm only a small change for them in a world of new forests, but I shouldered the weight as if it were a planet. That morning when I heard a curlew here, I coiled my fingers around the gate and strained beneath that final legacy. And I could almost see an old man standing in his dressing gown beside me with his ear cocked to the unlit sky.

The curlew's call stirs up deep wells of pleasure. Any bird can make you smile; it's fun to hear a lark or a clowny grouse, but a curlew prods you deeper, and it's more than jolly. The sound walks that spider-line between pleasure and pain, and it conjures up your old connections. Wullie lived a long life beneath a dynasty of wild birds. I bet their songs woke half-forgotten things in him: shadows of parents and lovers and the solemn throb of spring. But I loved curlews when I was a boy and had few memories to call upon. That's the curlew's special gift; they'll wake you to a web of old feelings and it doesn't matter if they're not your own. You smile and shudder in one fell swoop, and the day is changed.

So they're keenly precious birds, and the final pairs are dearer than all that came before them. The bond between people and wild birds is never simple, and we've been pressing our own ideas onto curlews for a thousand years. The Gaels called them *guilbhron* and said they were the voice of the restless dead. It was bad luck to hear a curlew calling in the darkness, and because of this our love grew cool and wary. We were trying to be good Christians, yet the sounds stirred memories of a ghoulish past. And the Church carved a deeper groove in curlews when the English Civil War came to Scotland in the seventeenth century.

The Stuart kings wanted to be head of the Church, and Galloway folk were stunned by the arrogance of it. It wasn't long before south-west Scotland was lit with rebellion again. Local folk made a puritanical covenant with God at Greyfriars Kirk in Edinburgh, and they refused to put up with the king's blasphemy. Declarations of defiance were nailed up, and Galloway gathered an army which marched on the capital. Of course they received a foul hiding for their trouble, but the point was clear: 'Don't tell us what to do.'

That was just the beginning. Government troops were unleashed into the south-west, and the Covenanters were hounded into the hills. Six thousand Highlanders were sent down from Perthshire to stun us with grand gestures of barbarism. They raped and pillaged and called it 'the Killing Time'. Dark days abounded. One fat Dumfriesshire laird used to hunt and kill the Galloway folk with wolfhounds, and he bound two women in the sea to drown at Wigtown. His name was Robert Grier of Lag, and they say the devil himself rode up the Solway in a coach and horses to carry him away when he died.

Grier of Lag refused to bury the bodies he left behind him. He meant to dishonour the Covenanters by leaving their bones to whiten in the wind. But without a grave, the dead men multiplied. We remember far more folk than ever died in the Killing Time, and we start to imagine that every ripple in the ground might hold the bones of martyrs. They say that two men were killed on our hill, but there's no stone to mark them and no way to learn the truth.

Harried and pressed to the point of death, the loyal Covenanters refused to attend church services held by the king's clergy. They shrank away into the hills and held secret ceremonies in the heather while the clouds and the rain scudded by. The soldiers hunted out on the moss for those meetings, and they'd post men on the high ground to watch for suspicious folk. Curlews have sharp eyes too, and they'll rise up and scream their name at any intruder – 'curLOO' carries far across the open ground – and so the soldiers would use the curlews to guide them. Many Covenanters became martyrs when the birds betrayed them, and it was only logical for Galloway folk to call them Satan's tools, servants of the hated foe.

Unable to wreak their revenge on the king's dragoons, the Covenanters poured their fury into the curlews. Eggs were shattered and the chicks were torn to shreds. Folk would spit to hear the curlew's call, and the rift was years in the healing. The birds soaked up this battering without a shudder of ill-will, and they flew on until we forgot the bad blood and loved them again. The odd squabble's normal when you're neighbours, and now a curlew's call comes to us like a fondness. But perhaps something never healed, and maybe that's what moves us when we hear the calling birds above.

*

Hill farmers spend the short winter days in the company of their livestock. The moors are frozen in the long night, and there's a sense of cabin fever. Maybe that's why curlews bring such a surge of pleasure when they come. Their songs remind us of summer days, of grass and lambs and restoration. Even the grimmest, ham-fisted hill shepherd will feel something flip in his chest when the curlews come home. Talk turns to summer, and folk start to feel optimistic. There's time to read the birds for omens; an early return foretells a good spring and settled weather, while late curlews bring nothing but ill.

When the weather finally turns and it seems like spring is on course, curlews begin to play out an ancient game. There are territories to define and partnerships to rekindle. I lie behind the dykes and listen to the male birds as they move in slow, mesmeric circles around the old calving fields. The displays are best heard at first light with heavy eyelids and the stars dribbling away into dawn. The birds call in a soft and sober moan for a partner:

whoo-UP whoo-UP whoo-UP.

They fly round again and stake their claim on some imagined line. Later, when the sun has risen, they'll tower up to perform long, delirious glissandos on set wings – that foamy trill is perfectly sublime, but it's just one of many songs in the curlew's repertoire. Hushed and almost shady, these predawn 'whoops' have made a lasting impression on us. The sound has given us the idea for another name beyond the universal 'curlew'. We call them 'whaups', and the word is a neat and cosy fit. But whaup is falling out of fashion in Galloway as the birds decline. Nobody says it much these days. Whaup has become a sound that old people make, and it withers away as time passes. Besides, things collapse at such a rate that soon we'll look back on all the names we had for birds and wonder why we ever needed them.

There's plenty of space for hope in the last days of March, but all's not well. The curlew's return has become a crooked and mournful thing over the last thirty years. Their numbers trickle away, and our first reaction on hearing a bird is often relief that they're still here. But at the rate they're going just now, they'll be gone in a decade.

There's no single nationwide cause for the collapse of curlews. It's more like a blend of problems has conspired to bring them crashing down with a sickening bump. We can't find any evil force which consumes the birds and drives them into extinction. It's just a steady and relentless failure to breed, and this stacks up year after year to spell disaster with the tragic certainty of a leak. I've watched 111 nesting attempts in various places across Galloway over the past eight years. Only twelve have survived long enough to produce chicks. Only one chick survived to fly.

Of course I was glad to see curlews coming back to our farm, and the early days of spring purred past in giddy joy. But there were would be many problems in the coming months. A return is just the start, and it's no guarantee of progress.

*

Sanny had been waiting for some reason to come and visit. Inspiration failed him in the end, and he just came anyway. He pulled into the yard as I was splitting logs, and the dogs jumped up to the window of his van and raked their claws down the paintwork. People hate that, but Sanny wasn't bothered.

His first act was to point out his house on the far side of the river. He said, 'That's me down there.' His is one of four lights we can see at night, and telling me that, placed a toe in the door. Our conversation was underway. Of course, Sanny already knew everything about me, so there was no point in my telling him. He'd hoed turnips for my father and he had some tales to tell about the Group Captain, my grandfather. He talked about himself and the things he knew instead – long, easy stories which bubbled up through the boards of a busy life. I guess he was seventy when he first came up to the house, but he was stronger than me and liked to say that he'd forgotten more about tractors than I will ever know. When I knew him well enough, I'd reply that forgetfulness is a cruelty of old age and Sanny would laugh through the gaps in his teeth.

When Sanny first retired, he used to stop in at the other farms in the glen. He'd get the crack and lend a hand, but everybody seemed to get busier and he fell out of the loop. He began to stay away from busy places because he didn't want to be an obstacle, but he was happy to drag me out from my computer because 'that's not real work anyway, son'. Most of his best stories came from the seventies when he worked for Jim Paterson at Tormannoch. 'Christ, he was some boy, Jim!' Sanny spooled out his tales and retold them a week later when the details had changed. I heard at least five different takes on the time that Budgie Carson shot a salmon. Some were better than others.

Sanny's tales were broken up with long wells of silence. He'd finish one story with a flourish, then he'd stare at the fields and let the gulls pass over him as they moved out to sea. At first it seemed like words were failing the old boy, but then I realised that silence gave him peace to cud the latest bellyful of chat. If things were up to Sanny, he'd have leaned on the dyke by the kitchen and smoked hand-rolled cigarettes all day long. My wife fumed because he ate all her biscuits, but he seemed to recognise her sacrifice and always deferred to her as 'Mrs Laurie'. He would also reduce his use of foul language by about eighty per cent when she was in earshot.

It was Sanny who showed me how to find satisfaction in grease and oil. He'd been a tractorman for many years, and he was thrilled by my David Brown. My generation believes that broken things should be discarded or replaced, so it was an odd novelty to be shown that repairs and improvements are possible. Sanny said I was part of the 'throw-away generation' and he despaired of me. It was unusual for him to offer direct help, and he preferred to explain what had to be done. I think he knew that was better than help, and he took my modest learning to a new level.

There was a day when Sanny came up and I was busting my shoulders on a nut for the sump. I couldn't get the damn thing to shift a quarter-inch turn, and the spanner seemed to have been set in granite. Sanny sighed and tutted and pulled up a length of scaffolding pipe from the gutter. He slipped the pipe over my spanner and made the lever longer by three feet. It was easy to undo the nut after that. I'd spent half an hour straining, but Sanny just said 'don't work hard, work clever', and rolled himself a fag. I'd always reckoned that most engineering problems could be solved by brute strength and ignorance. That's why I was so bad at it: I was weak and ignorant. Sanny made a decent case for 'weak and wise'.

But for all his backup and support, Sanny also nudged me on things I didn't like. He was happy to burn tyres and tip junk into the hedge. He had a story about dumping sheep dip into the burn, which killed everything for a mile downstream. He'd always been a keen fisherman, but he seemed not to make the connection. I was born to be anxious of burning tyres and the sloshing piss of diesel as panacea for a thousand farmyard problems. Just chuck some diesel on that, son; soak her in diesel and she'll come up fine. There's nothing here that a gallon of diesel won't fix. But that diesel will scar the earth with poison and it'll endure for years. It's easy to romanticise the old ways, though many of them were dire.

I showed Sanny some pieces from my Galloway archives. I'd built up quite a heap by that stage. I had files of newspaper clippings and letters from the local shows; there were ticket stubs and rosettes from New Galloway and Carsphairn, and I even had a dried-up curlew's egg from somebody's disbanded collection. It'd been gathered from the moss near Balmaghie in 1927, and the shell was almost white. I thought it would stir up old memories in him. Sanny took one look and laughed. 'Christ, son, what are you doing with that heap of junk?'

*

A cow's punch pans you and turns your guts black. My first time came on a wet day in the spring when the beasts were turning back into their pen. I was in a hurry, and one of the heifers wouldn't walk. I could've read the signs, but I was green and blind with rain and I never saw it coming. I tapped her on the tail with the palm of my hand and her hoof came up into my hip like a piston. I suppose I only had myself to blame, but that was no help as I rolled in the shit and cried at the drab horizon.

That hammering baptism was the first of many lessons as the beasts towed me into their world. You can't push Galloways. The old hills called for tough, resilient beasts, so we bred them to have a mind of their own. Press too hard and they'll turn away or stop altogether. Stopping is worse because it means you've pissed them off and they're ready to argue. Commercial breeds are dull and pliable by comparison. Character was weeded out in the search for speed and compliance.

It is easier for a camel to pass through the eye of a needle than for a herd of Galloways to move against their will. Rush it and you'll fail. Rage and you'll fail, so you coax and train them, and find the leading beast. Win her to your plan and the herd will follow. It's all political, and the animals move in a web of connections. You can read where they'll go before they've lifted a hoof because the weight will shift and the ears will turn. It's a mute broadcast, the sum of a hundred small details.

Sometimes there's a wild cow with a spark of madness in her eye. She'll freak and stray from the team, and that panic will wreck the flow. One reluctant beast can knacker your day and send the herd rumbling into the cloud. Movements must be made with a light and guiding touch; you propose an idea and plant the seed of your plan. If it doesn't work, just walk away and try another time.

This took time to learn. I strained at first because the beasts were a jumble and they wouldn't obey me. I'd blast them with curses and tore the shirt off my back in fury, but my anger just thrilled them and it made them worse. They'd tumble away into the whins and the wood would crack and shatter about them. I'd shake with rage, and it wore me out. I'd never come up against anything so stubborn and unmovable. I began to whine and plead for a bargain like a brat. That was the final straw. They've got no use for a snivelling wimp, and their sneers were biting. I loved those beasts, but I had no feel for them at all.

My first investment had been cautious. I'd left myself open for a quick exit, but even with the weight of fury and frustration, it was hard to imagine life without farming. I'd jumped, and I never stopped falling. More cattle soon came, and our herd expanded. My wife and I were both promoted at work, and we could afford it. The farm grew, and we ploughed our wages into the land. We had a deep barrel to fill before any profit could overflow. It would take many years to release our money again, but I relished the investment because I believed in every inch of the project.

*

But still we lacked a family. Three years had passed without the faintest glimmer of progress, and expectation was shifting towards doubt. We shrugged and wondered what the problem was. We were both hale and fit, and there was nothing to explain it. Luck just wasn't with us. The idea fell to a low, gnawing grumble in the back of my mind, but it was hard to measure the absence because I couldn't get a clear idea of what we were aiming for.

I was the youngest child of a large family and grew up as the kid. I didn't hold a baby until I was almost thirty. I thought it would be a watershed moment for me, and I listened to the safety briefing as the little girl was handed over. I was in the middle of thinking 'she's just like a puppy' when they took my picture, and then I gave her back again. The photo makes me look like some doomed presidential candidate.

So I had never longed for a baby of my own. I don't know many boys that do, and I suppose I feared the scat and bellow of parenthood which seemed to have befallen my friends. I heard some newly married couples speak of quiet yearning and readiness, but I was geared up to think that babies drop off you like rain from a wet coat, and you roll your eyes and groan 'not again'.

Older family members couldn't disguise their curiosity – 'Is she pregnant yet?' [nudge] or 'You'll be thinking about starting a family soon?' [wink]. Comments like these had always been a bit embarrassing, but now I found them irritating. I wondered what the old folk would say if I snapped at them and said, 'No, we can't have children and we don't know why, and it cuts into us like a knife.' One couple we knew managed to lap us and produced a second baby in less than three years. Some new maturity overtook them, and they only had time for the most absurdly boring conversation. They said, 'You'd understand if you had kids of your own,' and I thought that was pretty damn smug, even if they didn't know how it hurt us.

We had to adjust to change in every friendship we had. Kids seemed to hunt down our friends one by one and drag them into absence. We waited patiently, but I couldn't bear to tread water in my thirties as my life began to hurtle by. We sent christening gifts to the children of friends, then turned back to the farm and shut the gate behind us.

That left me with the weight of my archive, the recordings and the crates of newspaper which I'd gathered round me like a ring of wagons on the prairie. Some of it had been useful when I tried to plough and work old machines; most of it was just chats and tales with tough, gentle folk. I'd gathered them because they felt important, even if I couldn't see why. But they would be useless without a successor to take them on, and I began to feel like a block in the ditch with a swelling weight of memory at my back. My great-great uncle was rich, and he farmed all the ground around Lairdmannoch. His final years were frantic with gloom because he lacked an heir. He felt like his life's work would be doomed without one. My world is different in a thousand ways, but I can feel him.

Then I met Tam. At ninety-five years old, Tam had lived his entire life in a small cottage on the edge of rough country. As a young man, he'd been called from cattle into forestry work when the government bought the hill ground for planting and began to manage the ancient herds of red deer. Galloway stags are some of the biggest in Scotland, and it was Tam's job to fetch home their shot bodies. The stalkers would mark the fallen stags with a wrap of white fat around their antlers, and Tam would hunt the bodies out against the heather and bog myrtle. Some of the stags were so big that he would have to pull them out using a Clydesdale horse and a web of harnesses.

Tam's tales made my head swim. His slow, melodic voice was a livewire connection to a lost world. You don't hear the old Galloway accent much these days; most local folk have a simple burr which might be at home from here to Kilmarnock. I hung on every scarce and gentle flex in Tam's vowels. He sat beside a peat fire and smiled at me over his mug of tea. We talked of stags and bulls, and I promised to return the following week with a tape recorder. I had to capture every syllable he spoke. I phoned Tam to arrange my next visit and found that he'd died two days after I met him. He'd taken his old world into the ground with him.

Tam's death flattened me. I'd missed the chance to gather something of him, and now it was wholly gone. But the following night, when I stood in the shelter of my cattle, I remembered the dead man speaking about the dark hills beyond. I suddenly found my footing again. Tam never made an archive of his own life. Sanny thought the whole thing was daft. Those men had just lived, and the place came into them uninvited. I knew that if I could sink into my cattle and belong to them wholeheartedly, I'd see more of the truth in this place than any lifetime spent crooning at old clippings and photos and snatches of the long gone. I went home and turfed most of my albums into the attic.

*

Hill cattle survived for a time beyond the advent of modern European beasts because they were doing a job that Limousins and Simmentals could not. Heavy continental breeds grow quickly, but they can't stomach rough grass and the cold weather sickens them.

Galloways thrive outdoors and they're designed to be tough. That thick, double-layered coat pays dividends; there's no better protection against dull weather and cold. The beasts are highly prized in Canada and the American Midwest, where they take winter more seriously than we do, and it's hard to imagine the weather that would faze them. In fact, Galloways are so wedded to the bare sky that they often struggle with life indoors. They get sick, and their feet give out on concrete floors. Farmers who bring Galloways into their sheds during the winter often have to shave their backs to let the sweat come out, otherwise the beasts begin to slump with pneumonia.

Galloways grow slowly, but they're cheap to keep if you've got the right kind of hill ground. Imagine 'horses for courses' for cattle; European beasts were shipped in to graze the better ground whilst hill breeds were left to their own devices. This might've been the new order of things, but the value of old-fashioned beef carcasses steadily dropped until they couldn't repay the work required to manage them. You'd make less on a Galloway after three years than you could on a commercial cross at two. Government schemes recognised the value of hill cattle and offered subsidies, but still, it was tough work in lonely, awkward places. Younger folk were less fond of hard living, and Galloways became a project for old farmers who couldn't imagine life without them.

Then BSE bashed our confidence in British beef. The crisis tipped the balance away even further away from native breeds because the disease was linked to nervous tissue and was worse in older cattle. Emergency laws restricted the sale of beef from cattle over thirty months old, and it took a decade to lift that ban. Even now, animals which are over thirty months need to have their spinal column removed before butchering. Farmers have to pay for the extra cost, and it's no small trifle.

So thirty months has become the deadline for a fat animal's life. It's unprofitable to keep a beast for even a day longer. But Galloways were designed to be fattened over several years, and there is a clique of top chefs who all agree that the best beef comes from beasts at seven or eight years old. Now it's impossible to make money on a carcass like that, and slow breeds are utterly hamstrung by their refusal to grow quickly.

There's an old saying that Galloways can survive on fresh air and a fine view, and there's some truth in the sentiment. Left to their own devices on a patchwork of rough, varied grassland, Galloways will steadily grow into a fine, marbled carcass. But nobody can afford to wait that long anymore, and farmers rush their cattle with rich grass to beat the thirty-month deadline. Farmers laugh at the suggestion of 'fresh air and a fine view' as if it can't be done.

Hill cattle are scarce these days, and most of the moorland grazing has been given over to sheep. This seems like a straight swap, but sheep can't pick up the slack and they've driven an even steeper change in the hills. The land became poorer and the freshness flowed out of it. Sheep have begun to accelerate change in the hills, and now they get a bad name as wreckers and woolly maggots. It's unfair to blame them, and they miss cattle more than anyone.

Sheep and cows used to work beautifully together. The two overlap in a steady rhythm of mutual back-scratching, and one supports the other. Cattle like long grass and sheep prefer it short. Cows do the heavy lifting and sheep follow up with the details. If you can strike the right balance, the two will tackle the grass as it comes and keep the land in a choppy, buzzing balance.

Remove the cows, and sheep are restricted. They don't have the clout to punch into thick grass, and they're shut out of bracken. They focus their attention on the easy and accessible areas and hammer these into a billiard table. There's nothing left to hide a curlew's eggs. Other places are harder to reach, and they grow rank and tall without any grazing. The grass stands above your head, and then it's too rank for a curlew to land. The place falls oddly still.

GRASS

April

Warm and smirry darkness. A pair of curlews bond above the river and the drooling moss. I walk to the back field in my pyjamas and the rain swirls around me half-fallen. I'm carrying a bundle of hay as if it were a teddy bear, and I knuckle my eyes and yawn.

I want to find the bull. I think he's doing well, and he lays down fat and muscle with every passing day. I love the hump in his neck and the sweeping line of his shoulder. His appetite is growing, and we need to push his limits as the grass comes in. He must be firing on all cylinders, and I pour my energies into him.

He has slept the night beneath a birch tree, and he stands with a crackle as I come. It's dark under the drooping twigs, and I watch his white markings rise and stretch as birds sing on and water clicks in the mud below my boots. Then he bowls across the wet rushes to pull out my hay. I rub his neck and stand back in the half-light. He looks like an old-fashioned dinner guest in black tie, smart as paint. Tufts of his coat are being cast, and the linnets come to pluck bundles of white hair from his rigg. Their nests are in the myrtle where the new growth is foamy and rich.

The rain is sweaty, and a cuckoo calls out on the hill. He is the first of the year, and he pulses that news over the land like some Congolese fever dream. I can smell the jungle on that bird, and there is something vague and foetal in his stuffy double drum. Later when the sun is high I will watch this bird being thrashed by pipits and warblers as he paddles grandly through the willows. They hate him for a vagrant traitor. He will gape and snarl at them, and I will remember what it's like to know your home but have no place in it.

The grass came slowly at first. It was nipped by the frost and struggled to grow. Then a green haze came onto the hill, and the cattle gathered round in awe. Things looked good until an easterly wind crashed that progress into a standstill. But now there are warmer days and the green tongues begin to show again; the beasts hang back up the hill when I come with their silage because nothing can trump the appeal of fresh grass. I used to hold them in the palm of my hand at times like these, but now they stare at me as I clatter through gates and drive mud bubbling under my wheels. I am becoming redundant. Here is the real tipping point between the years – the moment when last year's feed is gently overtaken by fresh growth. When I was a naturalist, I recorded the dates of the first hawthorn buds and the sprays of cottongrass flowers. It was a hobby. Now I measure the spring's progress in pounds and pennies – every day without growth gnaws into my wallet.

I forget that this grass will soon be measured by the ton. Every slender blade feels precious, but it will rise in a torrent to bend heavy machinery. The dyke bottoms will be lost in nettles and docks and wet, rich grass. We'll end up wasting it and drowning in the surplus, just as I'll end up squandering the daylight which I longed for all winter. I'll sleep through the early dawns and the shallow nights with drowsy extravagance.

And now there is warmth at last, a scorching glare which makes the distance dance. Heather blurs into the birch trees, and the hill sputters. The beasts gather to drink from a deep steel trough and gurgle up threads of drool which blow in the wind like gossamer. The grass is beginning to swirl in eddies around their legs; soon it will tickle their bellies and lap away the rank clods of mud which trail below them. Heavy knees are sluiced in the soft rain and they come up clean and white. Hooves emerge like neat and waxy nuts.

They are heavy now. I visit them in passing, and for a moment I glimpse the movement of a calf under a heavy hide – a squirming flutter like a baby's kick.

Their guts are full, packed tightly and lolling to one side with a strange, uneven load. A hare has already dropped her young in the ditches below the cattle. We watch the leverets clustering around her teats in the gloaming. We call them 'mapsies' in Galloway, and we strain our ears for the 'map, map, map' of sucking.

*

Follow the river back to where it begins. Leave the salt mud behind you and run up the wide plains where the current pools in round and sliding loops. Go by the town and the hollow quarry, then break away from the flow. It's not hard to slide upstream through dank moss and the mould of a thousand oaks. Soon you're above the trees and riding up the bed of a neat and doughty burn. This high land is levelling, and the sky runs off like a rising tide.

You've done a trip of ten miles, and now you can turn and look back. The sea is flat and drab on the horizon, and land falls away towards it like a crumpled mat. There's a cool and lasting emptiness in this open space. The horizon comes in subtle lines, and the cloud-shadows run over them like a beast's breath.

And there we are, three decades ago, my entire family spread out and working. We stand against the far clouds and there is nothing but open hills and black cattle above us. The grown-ups pick stones from a ploughed field and heap the rocks as the sun turns above us. I'm too small to do much but scrabble in the ditches and hunt for frogs, but now and then I'll come to gape at the heaps which rise in the field corners. Some of the stones are bigger than I am; the clearing work is a job for heroes.

Today it's warm enough to go barefoot, and then it's lunchtime and others come with baskets of food. I worship the strength of my father and grandfather, but my mother and her friends excel in more practical ways. They bring food in superabundance, and the moss is decked with scones and cakes and flasks of tea. There's been a litter of collie puppies in the yard, and the shepherd's wife brings two of them up to play. I run with one until we're both dizzy, then we all go to swim in the burn and douse the heat in dark, amber pools of running water. I shriek in my pants, and dragonflies coast above the gurgling flow like helicopters. My mother has a ball of wild cotton in the band of her hat.

Clouds roll, and then we sit and spy the land below us for half an hour before work begins again. I'm fiddling with the buttons on my undone shirt, and I'm shown the house that my great uncle John squandered away with drink and bad debts. And there's the lane where my grandfather had his dog stolen. It was running along behind the tractor and a car slowed down and somebody opened the door and the dog jumped in and the car just took off and was gone. I clutch my borrowed puppy tightly. We look to the drowsy silhouette of Screel and Bengairn, two hills from the same root which stand above the bay. They used to say that Screel and Bengairn worked together to knit the weather in Galloway, and clouds piled up on the high ground when the needles were busy.

And we see the rising hills towards Gatehouse and Dalry. Those are grand, fearsome fells with hungry names like the Dungeon and Benyellary. I'm told you can still find ghouls and the wail of wolves in the scree of those places, and it makes me shiver to think of it. I'm supposed to be a man now, but still there's something cool in the dark shapes and the hanging spell of jittery birds.

We lounge in the long grass and I clamber over my family. I'm too small to read the quiet bump and tug between them. My father and grandfather are dissatisfied, and the two men strain against one another. The hills make room for the spread and clash of succession, but all I see is collie pups and the clutching moan of dog-stealing monsters in the distant fells.

We come off the hill in the evening light. The field is clean and bare in the gloaming, and soon the digger will come to renew old drains and make new ones. The whole lot will be reseeded and the land rescued from idleness. We are part of something much bigger, and farming was gathering pace in those days. The hills were being reimagined, and there were calls for more grass and faster food.

There are five gates to open as we come off the hill. That is my job. I kiss the collies goodbye, then ride on the Land Rover's bonnet and am ready for every gate along the way. Some are looped with baler twine; others have to be lifted up because the hinges are away. My grandfather reserves the right to drive and salutes me as he passes. I burst with pride, then I jump back onto the bonnet and cling to the windscreen wipers as we rush along two parallel streaks of tarmac. I never admit that it terrifies me.

My grandfather grew up in a jungle of moorland. The farmers of his generation worked in a web of meadows, hills and hayfields which had been carved out of the wild over centuries. That old system was handmade for cattle and wild birds. Heavy, lumbering beasts kept the whole landscape ticking over, and they drove a swell of diversity. Cows wrap their rough blue tongues around the grass and pull it up in a slow, ripping tug. Listen to a cow eating rushes: it's a murderous squeak of destruction like the sound of trainers in a squash court. The sloppy gobs are too big to worry about fine details, so they rake up thick draws of stuff with every grasp.

Then they move on and leave drooling gaps in the undergrowth. It doesn't take long for these gaps to fill with wildflowers and fresh new grass. I love to say the names of old wildflowers which grew here. Imagine Mountain Eternal and Bittervetch; picture Whorled Caraway and Autumn Gentian; extend your sympathy to the Melancholy Thistle. You could concentrate on wildflowers for a lifetime and still fail to recognise every species which grew the old meadows. Botanists came to study our fields in the 1940s. They often found fifty different plant species in a square yard.

For cows, grass is the fuel and ballast of life. It's plain to see how that connection works, but curlews have a different take. They don't eat grass, and they're drawn to the fields by a thirst for worms and spiders. The best grass was the older, cattly kind where variety was king. Life sprang up in the hoofprints, and exciting things happened when spatters of cow shit clattered down at random into that ancient salad bowl. Beasties filled the muck, and flies trolled the steamy pats. Curlews made their nests in the tussocks, and their chicks were embarrassed by the wealth of scuttling things.

For all their scientific intrigue, those old meadows were slow and steady places to earn a living. They were made for ponderous cattle with sturdy bellies. But life was about to speed up. Faster breeds need richer grass, and we couldn't afford to wait a second longer. Just when the hills were rusting into stillness, the better ground was suddenly gathering speed. The ancient balance was about to be sorely upset, and curlews stood on the edge of disaster.

The old, clattery meadows were reinvented. We sowed the land with new ryegrass species were which were hybridised to treble their nitrogen content. Then they were trebled again, and soon they were so rich and fast that there was no need for any other species. A modern field of grass might have three species in a square yard. The lush, sprawling growth is a superfood for fast-growing cows, but there's no room for curlews in a field today. The insects have gone, and the birds find it hard to place their eggs where the ground is even and clear. Besides, the crops are rolled and fertilised, then mown and mashed. Many curlews try to breed in the new grass-lands, but their eggs are slashed into ribbons or flattened by heavy rollers.

I learned all this theory in books at school. I turned the pages and felt a surge of horror because this change was the backdrop to my childhood. I gambolled and sprang through the hills as my family overhauled them. Suddenly our curlews were gone, and it was tough to stomach the idea that we were to blame. Our problem was that we couldn't afford to stand still, and my father had to make money. He took something that should've gone to curlews and gave it to me. It's not as if he saw that as theft because the birds could always go somewhere else. Reseed this land or plant that hill and the curlews will just move if they don't like it. It never occurred to us that we were taking everything.

So I stood and listened to their songs and heard a whisper of my own guilt.

*

The Highlanders loved to steal cattle. They made a game of it, and the never-ending play of raids and counter raids kept them busy. Sometimes they'd come to the Lowlands and lift cattle, but it's a hundred miles to Galloway and most of them preferred work closer to home.

The Killing Time brought the wild clans down into the south-west. They'd come to crush the Covenanters, but the strangers found other things to distract them in a land of fat cattle. They helped themselves, and many good beasts were spirited away into the night. But some of the Highlanders were dark, needling bastards who wanted more than beef. They smashed and raped their way across Galloway, and the south was shocked by the things they did. They passed so far beyond their orders that they became outlaws, and the Highland soldiers returned to Perthshire without them.

Those broken men moved into the hills between Galloway and Ayrshire and made a new clan of reivers and bandits in the steep granite scree. That's when cattle stealing really came to Galloway. The raiders would come down from the hills under cover of darkness, and they'd run the beasts away before anybody could stop them. Galloway farmers clubbed together, but the outlaws knew the value of speed and worked hard to whistle the cows into the trackless waste of wild country.

The way the land lies, there are only a few paths into the hills. Most were bound by tracks and paths, but the road which runs over the Old Brig of the Black Water was the surest way home for the raiders. The Galloway farmers knew that if they could reach that bridge before the Highlanders got to it, they'd have the chance to air their differences.

One night the raiders came and the farmers were ready. They rushed to the Black Water and lined the Old Brig with muskets. They'd fight to the death, and the men waited above the winding water beneath a glitter of stars. They heard their own stolen cattle driven towards them in the dark and began to fight.

Musket balls whirled in the night and the beasts milled in sad confusion, but it was deadlock. The farmers couldn't catch up their cattle, and the Highlanders couldn't force them over the bridge. That was when the outlaws fetched up a drum of pitch and set it on fire. They tossed that burning soup onto the herd, and the beasts were so mad with rage and pain that they stormed the bridge and tossed the defenders into the river. People say the outlaws rode those burning cattle across the bridge, screaming like demons and firing their pistols into the smoke.

It wouldn't be long until those bandits were rooted out and hung, but they left us one hell of a tale. And it rings so well in Galloway because only a Highlander could think of burning a live cow. That flair for drama has made them famous, but we've always taken cattle too seriously to risk their health on a piece of garish showboating. And maybe that's another reason why visitors drive past Galloway and head up to Perth and Fort William.

Even now, Galloways draw an enthusiastic following in strange and far-flung places. Some of the best animals are found in Yorkshire and Ireland, and there's a big market for Galloways in Germany. We've got little use for them anymore in a land without open hills and rough grazing, and while many do great work in wild country and hard mountains across the world, the beasts are just as easily reinvented as ornaments and show pieces for lowland parks. Americans call belted Galloways 'Oreo cows' because they say that black-white-black pattern reminds them of a biscuit they have over there. Whatever new guise those animals take, and whatever job they're asked to do, we deserve to be damn proud of our most celebrated export.

*

April came and drew swallows into the sheds. They chuckled and sang, then coursed away over the greening fields. The new grass was too rich at first, and it poured through the cattle like soup. They were drunk on the new growth, and I found them bucking and turning high-tailed to the hill. But it was hard for them when they lay down, and their grand bellies bound them to the ground. Sometimes they had to rock and bounce to help themselves stand, and when they were up, they stretched like old folk and groaned.

From the noisy chaos of the early-season days, a pair of curlews settled their nesting home in the rushes beyond the yard. I could see them from the kitchen window, but I was bogged down in the ploughed field which lay between us. I hardly saw them thrilling in the cold blue sun, but they sang over the house and turned their bellies above the line of our flapping laundry. My socks nodded their approval, but I was busy.

I'd chosen to grow oats in my first year. A cereal crop seemed to fit the new rotation, and I was drawn to the rush and bustle of the breeze through heavy seeds. We've been growing oats in Galloway for as long as anybody can remember, and the crop is a landmark for the people of Scotland. But I'd never seen a field of oats, and the decision was an act of faith.

In the days when I travelled around Britain to learn about curlews and farming, I found many places with less to show than Galloway. There are no curlews on Exmoor, and they're gone from large parts of Ireland. The birds have almost totally vanished in Wales, and only a few survive in Shropshire and Staffordshire, where a curlew features on the county's coat of arms. Waders rely on continuity. Their habits are a chain, and the birds return to their point of origin. Sudden declines shatter old traditions, and it's almost impossible to resurrect curlews once they've gone from a place.

But memories somehow endure. I worked with a farmer in Wales who felt the lack of curlews like a hole in his heart. He'd suffered for ten years since the last curlew came, and I followed his progress with cattle and plough. He'd built some of the nicest country you'll ever see for curlews, and it had become his life's work. I loved his enthusiasm, but I didn't hold out much hope because curlews had lost touch with that place. But one March came and a pair returned to his farm between the dark forest and the open hill. He called to yell that his curlews were back, and I jumped in the car to see his joy and the miracle of resurrection.

Sure enough, two birds walked through the rising grass, and we watched them in ecstasy. We made the pub thunder that night, and we stopped to listen for them in the gloom of Vivod Mountain when the bell was rung and we were turfed out in the darkness. Sadly, that lurch of progress was abandoned within a week. The birds vanished without ever laying an egg. There have been no other attempts in the seven years since.

I'd love to think that those birds were old timers paying tribute to the land of their birth. Maybe that's just whimsy, but the alternative is to think that they were youngsters, called back to that place by some genetic habit. If I were a scientist, I might explain it with fine points of geography or topography. Maybe waders are drawn to some places by things we cannot see. But those curlews soon realised their mistake and headed off to find success in a more likely spot. There are a thousand ways to read that return, but I can't resist the idea of shared memory, worn into their DNA like the shape of a comfortable boot. Maybe they felt something familiar in that place – the echo of ancestors.

A curlew's nest is a simple thing. It's a slight dip pressed into the moss and dressed with a few threads of grass. The eggs are a palmful, and they're laid one a day for four days to complete a clutch. The result is the finest picture of pointy-ended symmetry. The shells range in colour from a soft, creamy blue to shades of brown and green, delicately dressed with squiggled smears of pigment. Sometimes I find their nests by accident and look down as my foot swings into that bare cradle, a second from disaster. Then I spring away and torture myself with horrid notions of 'what if'.

It's hard for humans to find curlew eggs. Maybe we used to have the knack in the days when a nest meant food, but now we're clumsy and half-blind in the rough grass. You're hell-bent on staying upright and following some line through the cattle tracks, and you don't see much beyond the dull plod of your own feet. But foxes and crows have been whetting their skills for centuries. They watch for the sitting bird, and the corbies stand high in the trees at dawn when they know she has to stand or swap with her partner. A pair of curlews will easily see off a predator once or twice, but many crows and repeated attacks are hard to bear. Curlews need to win every contest and defend their eggs for almost a month. Crows only need to win once. And all the while a sitting bird can be rustled by a fox or a stoat. It's no wonder that curlews live for years in a restless hurl of motion. It's standing still that kills them.

Our curlews hooked an anchor on the earth. Having tumbled between the sky and the tide for many months, they laid their eggs and made a base in the rough grass. They bore the cost of that settlement.

I found a mess of feathers on the moss. They were dull and gummy in the rain, and the ends had been eaten off. Only a fox will bother to do that neat work, and later on he'll shit the quill ends to give you another hint. Crows might be interested in the eggs, but a fox wants the whole business, bird and all. You'll see him stand apart and watch for some small clue. Then he'll glide in through the long grass like an adder. Our patient, sitting bird will be gone and her eggs with her.

Curlews usually see the fox coming. If they're early in the sitting and the eggs haven't set into chicks, they'll often rise and fly away. But later on they'll try to hide because they've ploughed too much work into those unborn birds to risk losing them. They'll slow their breathing and try to hoard the scent around them. But the fox can follow the slimmest thread, and he'll always find his mark.

I've never seen it, but I think he comes with a pounce to stun the sitting bird. The eggs aren't going anywhere, so he has time to focus all his energy into death. Then he'll carry the corpse away and come back for the eggs, which he lugs in his mouth as if they're rare and special jewels. I've certainly seen him do this, and I've wondered at that strange angle of his jaw and the gentleness of teeth which have just been used to bust and puncture. He has cubs, and he'll show them how to lap at the yolks with their soft coral tongues. He's savage, careful and tender in the space of ten minutes.

In the days when these birds were strong, they took care of themselves. Curlews laid their eggs beside lapwings and oystercatchers, and they all shared the burden of defence. Beady eyes scanned the horizon for hunters, and the slightest intrusion was met with outrage. The birds worked as a team and drove off danger with fearless pride. Even the tiniest snipe will try to distract and confuse predators, and the shared impact can unman a fox. He'll lurk around the fringes where weaker birds make easy pickings, because he's also a coward.

Now that these powerful colonies have broken up into fragments, the mechanism has played out. Isolated birds are gullible and weak, and they lack the clout to protect themselves. The new forests are filled with watching eyes. The curlews come back to find their nests are empty and their work is wasted.

You can see the same pattern for people in the hills. Galloway used to be a famous place for good neighbours because folk knew how difficult life could be on your own. We made for a tough community because we worked together. Farms ran into one another, and folk reached their hands over wide moorland places. You did almost as much work on your neighbours' farms as you did on your own.

When my grandfather bought that hill farm in 1962, he found a shepherd to look after the place. The new man moved in with his family in the autumn, but nobody could've known how bad that winter would be. January brought eight feet of snow drifting into the yard and up against the byre doors. Hundreds of sheep were killed, and bitter winds raked the hill and razed the rocks to their ribs. The family was penned into the darkness, more than a mile from their nearest neighbours. It was a national crisis, and it nearly sank the government.

But they weathered the storm. My grandfather finally dug through to find them, but it was March before the ploughs could make it out there. Life began again, but snow lay up the dyke backs until midsummer. One cool day in May, a crate came up the road from the post office in Dumfries. It was simply addressed to 'The Occupants', and it was packed with jars and cans of jam and cherries and lemons. It'd come from a previous owner of that old hill place, a farmer who'd migrated to Canada a decade before. Five thousand miles away, he'd read about the awful storms and imagined how hard life would've been in Galloway. Without ever having met the new family, he packed up a crate of supplies and sent them over, because that's how you support your neighbours.

It's harder to stick together nowadays. There's not so much work going on farms, and life's too busy to stop and enjoy the folk around you. Things are easy if you have neighbours, but you need a stout heart to endure weeks of pale solitude in the middle distance. And maybe that helps to explain why our curlew's nest was emptied and the bird was taken.

The shells were carried away and gouged with holes; I found them lying beneath a favourite boulder where crows often stand. The rocks were spattered with white shite, and the parted grass revealed fragments of other eggs like dandruff – grouse, snipe, oystercatcher and skylark. There were sun-dried frogs and bits of lizard, glossy black pellets of fur and wool. This rotten debris was made lovely by the first wildflowers. Pink flakes of lousewort and milkwort ran rampant through the grass.

Incubation is the first awful chasm in the curlew's year. The eggs must be kept safe and warm for thirty days until they hatch, but this is hard work against the odds.

Curlews usually fail these days, and a large part of that failure belongs to us. They cannot fathom how we've changed this place and tipped their safety away from them.

*

People say that having children makes you think about the future. Not having children does the same, believe me.

My wife and I began to take active steps towards parenthood, and our discreet enquiries were met after a year with an official medical response: 'Don't worry, keep on trying!' So we did, until three more years had passed.

My wellies traipsed a clod of muck into the GP's surgery. He passed us on to Dumfries, so I littered that consultant's carpet with shreds of hay. We underwent tests and were prodded and explored from a variety of angles. Soon we faced fertility treatments and measures to provide 'assisted conception'. They don't do anything as fancy as this in Dumfries, so we were passed on again to Glasgow, where we sat with other couples in an airless waiting room.

I was felled by the jolting whack of that place. I'd been out in the moonset darkness that morning, drinking the smell of cattle in the stars. Now I was listening to feet squeaking on plastic flooring. I sat with the other wretched men, each of us pondering separately how it'd come to this. Our wives and partners were summoned, and we pored over a selection of nervily kneaded magazines and avoided eye contact with each other.

Lots of women came to the clinic on their own. I felt bad for them at first. You'd think their husbands could have come with them. Being involved was making me feel useful, but the truth is that men bring very little to this process. Women organised the appointments and took notes on injections and doses; they quizzed the nurses and understood every twist and turn of the protocols. Men toed the ground and made noisy, phoney jokes to reassure themselves. In the end, I began to think that the squeamish, maudlin sufferance of menfolk was a poor match for that molten fist of female determination. We were just something to lean on.

The entire process was explained to us. The nurse said, 'Most of this comes from research into AI in cattle,' as if that was a consolation to me. We sat in her windowless office in the bowels of a vast block of wards and consultation rooms. We were her last appointment of the day, and the corridors were horribly quiet. A strip light flickered, and I wondered if it was just my eyes getting tired. There were cattle to check when we got home, but those animals seemed a million miles away from the beige cube where we sat between a curtained bed and a door and a computer. It said WASH YOUR HANDS on the wall. I'd washed my hands, but I'd picked up black calluses of grease and oil which I couldn't shift. I put them in my pockets like a child in case the nurse told me off.

She talked us through the treatment and broke down the fertilisation process into a series of steps. She had a diagram of the female anatomy; the reproductive organs are shown from the front. When it's a cow, those organs are usually shown in profile. I wondered whether to point that out, but I caught my wife's eye and instead we smiled and nodded and took a bundle of leaflets which explained in excruciating detail how the next few months would play for us. As we left the nurse, I made a joke about the lovely day. 'What lovely day?' she said. We walked for ten minutes before we saw the sun.

Then we were home and out from a hot car and over the fields for a swim. The loch stood in a mug of hills and the water was clear and peat-deep. I was so used to thick jackets and self-defence that nudity was novel. I had a dark red vee in the crook of my collarbones, and my arms were white from the elbow up, but we looked like any other couple as we slid into the water. All the weight of that clinic had crumpled away in our clothes.

My wife is a born swimmer. You don't get far in Cornwall if you can't swim, and she had lifeguard training in a heavy sea. The first time I went to Cornwall I was flummoxed by that sea. Waves dash and hammer into the shingle, and the cliffs are sown with salt mist. My sea was the Solway and the surly glug of brackish mud, and those Atlantic waves clattered into me like falling timber. I watched her surfing from the shore and felt like I loved a mermaid. She was brown and freckly in those days before she came to live in the clouds with me.

She finds this loch easy, and she slips away from me like an otter. I follow the line of bubbles, and then she's back and turning with a broad, honest grin. I know how deeply she's suffered, but now she's a girl again, and the recollection makes me painfully proud of her. I want to go further out towards her, but I'm pathetic in the water. I bob in the shallows like a mouldy cork, and now she's out from the shore and gliding away through the loch. And when she comes back, she's confident and strong. I fall out of my depth and she laughs, and even the sound of it is safe.

Later we lie in the short grass and the sun comes to dry us. Talk is easy, and the greening hill runs high and far above us. The fretful trek to Glasgow had strained something between us, but now we're together again. I go back to my clothes and find an adder curling himself around my boot. Sanny killed every adder he saw as an expression of good citizenship, but we love to see them. He huffs like a cobra, then he glides away, and we walk to the house and the moan of grazing cattle. We've called that place 'adder bay' ever since.

CROP

May

The remaining curlew is baffled by his loss. He tries to find a new partner, and I lose him in the anonymity of the hillside. Even if he does find another female, it's hard to imagine how their chances will improve with repetition. Maybe the grass will be longer next time, and maybe the fox will pass them by. I watch them at dawn, flying round in loops and conjuring up fresh hope.

The neighbour has put heifers in the fields below us. Our bull is hooked, and he wails in heartbroken torment because there are three dykes and two fences between him and paradise. He jogs up and down the dyke until there is a muddy track of his hoofprints in the rushes. I go out to see him, but the visit is poorly timed. He's in a frenzy, and I am the focus of his excitement.

He tips his chin. There's a high, rumbling bellow, and then he charges towards me at full speed. Clods of soil fly up into the grey sky, and it's a wincing, twisting thrill to see him close the gap. He won't hurt me on purpose, but he can do plenty of harm by mistake. It's a game, but I must stand my ground and master him. My eyes widen and my knuckles turn white. He weighs 800 pounds, and I can see threads of creamy foam on his lip. I shrink and stomach the dizzy realisation that I am far out of my depth. If I am trampled, the nearest help is a mile away.

Fear comes to me like a stranger. I am used to comfort and ease, and I do not recognise this taut, jangling discomfort. Low clouds, panic and imminent pain.

We have friends coming to celebrate Beltane, so I have spent the afternoon building a fire. Here is the death of winter and the birth of new opportunities. Cattle are supposed to head out to their summer pastures at Beltane, and the symbolic fires cleanse the land of winter's ill. My beasts could have been moved a week before the first of May, but I held them back because I liked making that old connection. The Celts would dress their beasts in garlands of yellow flowers to represent fire and the purity of summer. I would probably do the same if I had time, but I have work to do. I make do with a sprig of whin flowers for the kitchen table, a gold and buttery bunch in a jam jar. The house smells of coconut, then I am in the yard bent over a collapsible power drive.

We have stepped away from friends in this place. The farm has pulled my wife and I away from our old connections, and now we go for weeks without seeing anyone of our own age. This life is lonely and isolated, and we lean heavily upon each other. I can understand why young people do not want to work with hill cattle anymore.

Soon it is dark, and the fire rises. Old friends have come and I am suddenly giddy; I draw deeply on their company, and I mix it with ale until the flames make the rushes dance in orange light. We laugh and try a dance, and my fingers cramp on the keys of our accordion. I am not used to fine and delicate movements these days; calluses blunder across the ivory keys, but enough people are clapping to convey the gist of 'Mhairi's Wedding'. Some of us were in a band at university and others improvise. A friend from Campbeltown says he knows how to play the spoons, but when we clear him some room for a solo, the clatter is metreless and weird. The tune falls around him, and he leads the laughter.

Soon we are left with the final stragglers; I stretch out beside the glowing embers and stare at the moon as the guests mutter and giggle. The sky has cleared and a curlew begins to sing above us. Curlews love still and moonish nights like these. I watch silver clouds piling up above the fells where Galloway runs into Dumfriesshire.

The curlew kneads the air from a dozen angles until he crosses the moon at last, and I am left with the impression of a searing silhouette; wings swept back like a sickle. I feel sure of a note of stubborn madness in the sound. I wish I had not smoked so many cigarettes; my head begins to pound as the air fills with slashing, throbbing birds.

*

The seed oats came in a half-ton bag. We couldn't get it off the lorry because we didn't have any lifting equipment. We finally solved the problem with a digger, but it recalled the nagging idea that I was trying to force a square peg into a round hole. Cereals belong in an arable world these days, and heavy lifting equipment comes as standard on modern farms. Mixed farming moved away from Galloway, and arable became a job for streamlined specialists. The delivery driver said he doesn't come this way much anymore. The cows bellowed at him as if he was a stranger.

Rain fell throughout April and made progress impossible. I began to feel antsy and impatient, but it's a bad idea to rush the steps towards sowing. As much as I raged against the heavy sky, I had to soak up the rain. Bowing to the unchangeable had become part of the job. Finally the clouds cleared and a cool, drying breeze ran over the furrows. I could hardly stand the suspense and rushed to harrow them, pulling the machinery into the crumbly soil. I'd bought some harrows and fixed them up, and I'd learned how to hammer rivets along the way. It's fun to work with a ball-peen hammer, watching the metal slowly melt under a hail of taps. The effort paid off and I wallowed in the powdery haze of dust which boiled up into the tractor's cab. Later that day I harrowed it again and was thrilled by the turmoil of grey breadcrumbs that I left in my wake.

Serious farmers drill their seed into the ground with precision equipment, but I was set to broadcast my crop from the muzzle of a converted fertiliser spreader. It's the old-fashioned way, and it saved me the cost of anything better. Seed flew across the field in thick sprays like confetti, then I pulled off the spreader and went back for the harrows again. Oats need to be buried beneath the soil, and the harrows helped to tickle each seed safely underground. With a final flourish, I rolled the crop with an old roller, something I'd borrowed from the scrapyard in the town. Then all the ingredients were there, mixed and stirred to what I felt was a state of near perfection. All I needed was rain, and it came the following afternoon.

The hill was dark with a coming storm; bruisy blue clouds piled up over the moss and pressed on my chest until my eyes were bulging. The air drooled like warm broth around the stagnant grass, and thick pieces of it came in through the byre window and lay upon me.

So I drove uphill to find my cattle and check them again for a calf. The pickup purred out across the moor, and the air swirled behind me in dust and the reek of powdery moss. My neighbour keeps a few of his cattle in this rough country, and I rounded another corner and found his tractor parked in the road, engine still chattering and leaking blue fumes into the dark sky. Chains trailed down off the loader and into deep reefs of bog myrtle and bracken in the verge. I could hardly read the scene at first, but then I saw the man himself sunk up to his knees in a slopping mess of peat. He was digging hard with a short spade, pulling up long sweeps of black peat chowder like a man baling out a leaking boat. I stopped the pickup and realised that he was battling at the flank of a beast which had sunk to her ribs in a hidden drain. She turned her head and moaned.

I saw long black eyelashes and soft, velvet ears. This cow was one of his best pedigree black Galloway heifers; home bred and the pride of his heart. I imagined one of my own heifers in a similar hole and the thought scared me. He reckoned she'd fallen overnight, and he'd done well to spot the dark shape in the verge as he passed. He might have driven by for days and then found her when the foxes began to pull black hair across the road and the retching stink lay like a dome above her ribs. Now she could be rescued, but this job was far from done.

A single chain was looped under her belly, then we worked together to slip a second under her breast to balance the pressure when the tractor began to pull. I was quickly black and sodden, and the sky rumbled over us until there was twilight in this narrow bend of the roadside. We'd trodden on the new myrtle and crushed up a fine scent from the spoony leaves, and we'd trampled the orchids and the bracken both with our digging.

Rain finally began to fall as the tractor took up the slack and the beast humped at the draw of the chain. Each of us was thick with falling water, and the heifer was hauled up from the black soup. Soon there was a crack of daylight between her belly and the mud, but she was weak and could hardly stand. We unhitched the chain and tried from a new angle, but then her back legs were free and the rain was battering into us and we saw her ankle broken and the mangled joint white as only fresh bone can be. It was busted when she fell, and the rescue had been doomed from start. He swore at the ground in a single, quiet spit.

Then thunder came, and he drove down for the vet. I sat with her and we bathed in warm rain together. Lightning split the glen in sheets and palls, and night seemed to come in the mid afternoon. The bog twitched with the patter of falling rain, and half an hour passed before the vet was there in a pair of glossy waterproof trousers. It took a moment to kill her, and then she was dead and her corpse was a burden. Rain spattered into her eyes and left a blue mist on her lashes.

We sat in the tractor's cab and smoked cigarettes in silence afterwards. I followed him home and watched the heifer towed back to the yard with her busted hock trailing behind her. Water pooled and gabbled in the hill tracks and rushed through the ditches to flush out the tadpoles like rabbits from the long grass.

And we stood together in the yard afterwards. The hill smelled clear and fresh, and cuckoos came to bell in a sorry sun. Galloways are hard, capable beasts, but they aren't infallible. We trust them to find their own way, so it hurts when they fail.

*

The smell of a fox. I'm moments behind him, and for a second I forget the weight of the cattle-trough on my shoulder. I forget my work and imagine that dark shape slipping through the bracken fiddles like a blade. I'm sure he's watching me from the high ground. He has run ahead and then turns to study me from a distance with his tail curled over his toes.

There's always a fox. You can't do anything in this place without his supervision. He'll run at first sight, but something in you will pull him up and he'll turn and stare in quiet fascination. A thousand times I look up and find that I'm being observed, and ten thousand times I never see that sharp enquiry but know it's there.

We can't read anything in that cool, yellow-eyed face, and he never gives the inch of a hint. So we live side by side and we dress him up with our ideas as if he were a mannequin. Some people say he's a devil and a tinker. Others make him a baby, with dishy eyes and a soul. But nobody's right, and nobody knows him.

Curlews weave amongst us, a fox can tie us in knots. There's light and heady baggage in the business of birds, but we love to be outfoxed. And we forget to question the truth when we hear tales of his latest adventure. A litter of small red collie pups was born at Dundrennan after the bitch ran into a dog fox in the rushes – there's a long tradition of this in Galloway, and the half-bred pups are called tod's tykes even though they're an impossible blend; a fox can't produce anything from a dog. And I hear there's a fox who makes a raft from the wracks of drifting seaweed so he can ride across the bay to hunt the island at Auchencairn. They're canny beasts.

Sanny's got a grand story about foxes. I've heard it lots of times, and it makes me smile from ear to ear. He was out fishing on the edge of darkness one night. This was in the days after the war when he'd just left school and found work at the knacker's yard in Gelston. He hated that job, carting dead beasts to be rendered, and he lit his first cigarette to cover the stink. Finding himself with an hour spare after work one evening, Sanny headed up to the loch with his rod for a quick look around. Sanny fished in all the best places back then (though you won't see his name in the official rod records; he was more of an 'after dark' fisherman), and he'd not been fishing long when a fox came along the riverbank towards him. 'Oh aye', says Sanny. 'Where are you away to?'

Born with an inbuilt loathing of foxes, Sanny shrank into the shadows and cursed the lack of something heavy and blunt in his hands. Given half a chance, he would've dumped a boulder on that fox and thought the job well done. The fox pulled up a few yards away and began to pull tufts of wool off the barbed-wire fence which ran along the water's edge to keep the sheep from the water. Sanny's murderous plans turned to curiosity.

The fox picked and tugged at the wool until it had a fistful of white fluff in its mouth. Sanny was baffled as the fox then turned round and began to walk backwards into the loch. Inch by inch, it slowly vanished into the shallow water, still holding the big ball of loose wool in its mouth. At the last possible gasp, Sanny looked down and saw only the little black nose and the ball of wool standing on the surface. With a final wink, the nose was gone and the wool was left to drift free. Following a stream of bubbles, Sanny was astonished to watch the fox re-emerge on the lochside and shake itself dry. Without a backward glance, the prowler returned to its beat.

I daresay that you'd have been just as stumped by this as Sanny was. A gentle breeze drove the sinking wool up towards Sanny, and he bent down to pick it up. But a sudden instinct caused him to lean in for a closer look first. He lit a match in the gloaming and found the sheep's wool was wriggling with every kind of flea, ked, tick and louse you could imagine.

They must've walked up the length of the fox as it sank into the water and finally found themselves marooned on a dead end. Of course Sanny was disgusted, and he dropped the match to spring away from the shipwrecked bloodsuckers.

And so Sanny learned at first hand how a fox keeps himself free of fleas and parasites. He told a friend who nodded sagely and said, 'Fancy that, Sanny.' But the friend was forgetful and bumped into Sanny a few days later and said, 'You'll never believe the shite I heard from somebody the other day: that a fox gathered up a dod of wool and walked backwards into the loch with it to clear himself of fleas – what a load of rubbish that is.'

To Sanny, the really outstanding thing about this story was that folk didn't believe it. It made no sense to express the many doubts I had. If it was that easy to get rid of fleas, why didn't we just wash them off? The story seems pretty fragile from a number of angles, and I was tempted to pull the rug out from underneath it. But then I realised that I could never change his mind or presume to correct the old boy. And there's space in this world for his truth and mine.

Who knows what he really saw? I heard the story so often that I finally began to believe it. Oddly enough, there are a few accounts of precisely the same thing happening in other places, but maybe that just proves that people like a good fox story. Gather a dozen old folk together and get them talking about the fox. After half an hour they'll be cheering and laughing at the wild cheek of him, and by Christ he's got a nerve! But if a fox walked into the room at that moment, he'd be torn to shreds.

Wullie Carson reckoned that killing foxes was part of his farm business. We found bundles of his old snares hanging in the rafters of the stables when we first came here. Some had seen action; the smooth wires were kinked with balls of faded fur. I turned up a fistful of gin traps in the pigsty, mostly rotted through and almost unidentifiable. Gin traps are a horrible way to do business, but they certainly work.

Wullie waded into the natural world because wildlife was a seamless part of his place; it was only right to keep an eye on it. People like Wullie made foxes scarce, and the ripples ran across open country. Curlews became common because the land was right for them, and they boomed because nothing lived to kill them.

Wullie's generation has died away, and foxes have come back. They love the new forests, and there are more of them than we ever knew in the old days. When curlews crashed, we rose to blame foxes because the long grass was littered with broken wings and ghosting feathers. Besides, we've been fighting foxes for years and we know a good scapegoat when we see one. But we planted the forests where the foxes live, and we tipped the grass out of balance so the curlews had nowhere to hide. How like us to pass the buck and blame the fox for all this sorry business of decline and collapse in the countryside.

Even the scientists agree that foxes are part of the problem; many of the big conservation charities have started to hire guns. There is good evidence that killing can rebalance the system for curlews, but it's a grim and sallow-faced thing. Some people call it predator control, but that's cowardice because there's no controlling a wild animal. They mean predator-killing, but that's no way to speak about wildlife. Of all the things that the curlew's call has meant to us over the centuries, now it seems to mean a blood cost, and the death of foxes. It's no longer merely the wild cry of open moorland and meadows, but equally the sound of calculated death and manual balancing. We can't kill our way out of this problem, but it's part of the answer, if we can stomach it.

I was ready for that work, but my memories hang around a fox we killed at Clonshank; it was almost twenty years ago. The terriers bore him up from his den in clouds of dank and rooty breath. Foxes are supposed to bolt when the dogs go in. The guns stood ready for that mad rush, but this boy wouldn't come, so we dug into the ground and pulled him up. There was no room for misunderstanding in that narrow slot of soil. He was rigid and bare, and we killed him in a mat of pine needles and spittle threads.

Pinned and hammered, the terriers came up and ruffed his dead scruff until it was rank and claggy. The little dogs were wired to the moon, but there was no fun in that job beyond that wild ecstasy of frothing dogs. If you need a fox to die, then here's the delivery of death. And it was hard for me to bear at first. It came back to me and burnt a hole where callus grew. I was less minded to blub or whine the next time we did it, but the job was never simple. I was toughened to this kind of work, but the fox was born ready.

I began to kill foxes alongside the farm and the cattle, and curlews came to help me. The birds have a special alarm call when they see a fox, and that sound becomes dispassionate and functional, a smoke alarm for rising fear. I would be wrapped up in some rough nook and would wake to the yickering scream of curlews. I'd reach for the rifle and squint into the gloom. More than one fox died because the curlews spied him first in the rising grass. I began to hear those warnings with a glow of relief – relief that a tired, uncomfortable vigil would soon be resolved one way or the other.

And in that moment when we killed the fox at Clonshank, another fox was surely watching us from the bracken or the sliding scree. His face would have been blank as the drab sky, with his tail curled over his toes.

*

Then hot weather came, and lizards skittered through the shelter of the old dump. They coiled themselves around rusting wheels and sheets of crumbling tin, their piggy tails twitching in satisfaction.

After days of secrecy, the oats came bursting out of the crumbling soil with indecent haste. The drab grey field bristled with creamy green fingers, and the contours showed in a haze. Soon it was possible to spot wrinkles and inconsistencies in the distribution of these seedlings and match them to errors I made when spreading the seed. Sanny was thrilled by the work, particularly because it gave him new scope to drily prod my flaws. Memories came flooding back to him, and he warned against pigeons and rabbits. Both should be taken in moderation, he said. 'It'd be a hard, thin world if you couldn't spare a mouthful of crop for the doos and coneys.' Both found their way into our kitchen in the lengthening evenings, and the dogs drooled to the scent of browning game.

There was a bustle of hushed excitement; the soil rose like bread and gleaming beetles scurried across the crust. A stonechat sang like a robin from the telegraph wire and blinked a beady eye at the rush and riot of swallows below. Thick, heavy clouds piled up on the horizon again, but I could feel the sun burning my arms as I mucked out the cattle shed and dumped the shitty straw in a heap where the foxgloves grow. This job would've taken half an hour if I'd had a front loader for the tractor, but I'd blown my budget when the radiator burst and was licking my wounds with a wheelbarrow and a grape. It was hard work, and the pissy nip stung my eyes. The chickens had been laying away in the old straw, and I turned out a nest of twenty eggs by mistake, yolks across the floor, briskly gobbled by the dog.

Impatient and keen to be done, I turned to the tractor and tried to hitch a bucket to the hydraulic arms. This would hurry up the job, but the steel frame was rusty and had to be pulled into place. I tugged and swore, and suddenly I was slipping on fresh grass and the horizon tipped away from me. I felt something tug my overalls and then my head thumped on the turf.

I stared at the sky and realised that I'd fallen onto an upturned silage spike; three feet of sharpened steel pointed diagonally into the sky. The metal point had passed through the baggy fabric of my overalls and now the shaft was kissing my side. I had a small bruise, but a few inches to the left and I'd have been gabbling in a froth of tepid blood.

I returned to the terror that night. I lay in the bed on my back with my hands clasped across my chest like a fresh corpse. The sun had shone all day on the wet ground and the house was filled with the gentle, powdery scent of peat and cotton. Curlews wailed beneath low cloud. I could hear my wife breathing. I puzzled over that looming spike and knew it as one of many threats to my life. I could be torn apart by a tractor's power drive or ground into splintered meal by a cow protecting her calf. A thousand ignominious ends beckoned me; I could die tomorrow morning in a fashion so ignoble and pathetic that the memory of it would be used to teach children in the school. I cradled my own brand of soppish terror, and I used it measure the distance between me and manhood.

I felt the weight of this place, carrying the baton for a brief moment in time. We found records of this place from the early 1600s, and now there was my name as the latest and least deserving in a fine strong chain. I was meddling with farming, telling myself I was being wholehearted. Suddenly I saw how pathetic it was to test myself against the heft and bellow of history. That silage spike hunted me in the darkness, dug out the fool.

I lay thinking about when we came to visit this place for the first time on a wild, sleety night in December. One of Wullie's family members met us in the yard and let us into the house. My wife's footsteps clattered around the empty rooms, and I listened to the story of the old boy's final hours.

He'd been lying in the hospital at Dumfries, then some fit or fever had taken him and he rushed home in confusion, determined to feed a dog that had been dead for a decade. I pictured his mad, tragic dash across the yard, an old man in his pyjamas, baffled and scared of this yard which had been his for nearly a century. It was a cruel end for him, but he had lived here for too long to suffer that supervised cooling which passes for death on the wards. His courage ran out into the stones, and death found him fumbling like a baby in the midst of all his tools and know-how.

Before we left, we had a look in the sheds. There were scythes and paraffin lamps hanging from the rafters in the byre, and I found a crate of his junk in the old dairy. I thumbed through and made a vague note of the contents: electric fuses, chisels, a tyre valve, medicine bottles, a packet of razor blades, pop rivets, a dosing gun, welding rods, castration rings, fencing staples, a coarse metal file, a broken metal file, batteries, a wiring loom for a trailer, two mouse traps, a bottle of iodine and a battery tester.

Like so many folk in this line of work, old Wullie could turn his hand to anything. Farmers might love growing plants or handling livestock, but you don't get far unless you can balance that skill with a knack for engineering or accounts. So feel for me, who excels at nothing worth doing and almost killed myself with sheer clumsiness.

This place has passed through too many hard and capable hands for it ever to be truly mine. Farming is fearsome, and unless I was very careful I'd soon be killed in some daft and laughable accident. People would tut and say, 'His parents should never have let him try.' But then I kicked against that wilting deference and knew that even Wullie would have been scared in his time. It's mad to be fearless, and maybe what I envied was the steady, measured mastery of danger. Perhaps that was something to aim for.

The hill poured warm scent in through the open window. The old boy had lain in this room and smelled that same land in the dark. Perhaps he'd been smelling it when he had rushed across the yard and his time had finally come. He'd been afraid then, but even that was a note of defiance and a thumbed nose to the doctors. I rolled over onto my side beneath heavy covers and stared into a well of inadequacy.

*

I thought our curlews would rally, but they stumbled into chaos. Most of them returned to the coast, but a few hung around the river and the low fields.

Feeling their absence, I took an hour to drive up the hill road to sit and watch for curlews in a favourite spot. This is rough heather country, thick with grouse and hawks. It doesn't belong to us, but it looms over this glen and casts a deep shadow upon us all. I found five white vans parked in the layby, and there was mud on the track. I looked to the higher ground and found the hill was oddly hung with black shadows. There were people spreading out across the land with bags of saplings; they'd come to plant this hill. A curlew rose to watch them in a long, slooping turn. His breast seemed to hang beneath the line of his wings like a pouch and his feet trailed behind him. The bird had no idea what the new trees would mean. He returned to the grass with a pretty flutter and a flare of his white arse.

The planting went on for a month. It's still too soon to see the new trees, but they'll bristle through in a couple of years and the hill will start to vanish. In the chequerboard pattern of Galloway, another white square turns black. I always thought this place was the last real stronghold for curlews in the parish. The other birds are merely fragments around this hub.

I heard that similar forests were planted in Ireland a generation ago. The landowners ploughed the moors and stuffed the cracks with trees like we did, but the people rose up and wouldn't have it. The new plantations were burnt out and vandalised, and it took a fair bit of work to get people settled down before the ground could be replanted. We're not so different from the Irish, and the people of Galloway have a habit of rebellion. The old Levellers might have looked for some gesture of defiance, but the truth is that the old world was damn hard and few folk could stomach it any more.

And foresters aren't the only people who like our hill ground. Twenty years ago we bore a fad for renewable energy which came down from the cities and left us whirling. Old hill roads were suddenly filled with land agents in branded gilets and businessmen with impractical shoes. They parked their shiny cars in stupid places, then unboxed new wellies for the short walk across the farmyard.

This was the boom time for wind power, and a dozen reps came our way and promised to make us rich beyond our wildest dreams. They unfolded enormous maps and read them upside down, and they couldn't pronounce the names of our places. They didn't seem to care that the plans they made were wild and undoable – they got down to business and they'd come to barter. They promised us millions and we said, 'That's crazy!', and they laughed and said, 'We know it is!' It all seemed like fantasy until we went back in the kitchen after they had gone and found the place still honking of expensive aftershave.

But then things started to happen. Incredible diggers arrived and tippers carted rock across the open hills. Teams of workers came out from somewhere and began to throw wind turbines into the sky. That's when it seemed a bit more credible, and folk began to sign up to agreements with companies with glossy names and strange ambitions. More turbines came, and soon the horizon was bristling with cranes and cables and flying white sails.

People started to get worried and complained about all this development to the council in Dumfries. There was a big sign that went up on the roadside near Kirkcudbright which said 'Bonnie Galloway or Windfarm Dump?', but most of those complainers were English people who'd just retired here and didn't understand that Galloway had always been a working place. The council wouldn't hear them at first, but then a hundred more turbines went up and they started to worry too. They had a word with Parliament in Edinburgh, and it was them who finally said, 'Change is coming and Galloway had better just get used to it.' And that's what they've said ever since, whether it's more trees or new pylons or another birling windfarm.

Government ministers sometimes come down and pose for photographs with industry bigwigs. They stand at the sawmill and wear plastic hats, and the papers say that Galloway is making leaps and bounds in forestry and renewable energy.

And all the politicians and head honchos hail from Glasgow and Edinburgh anyway, so we start to feel like we don't have a horse in this race and there's no point arguing.

We never signed up with a wind farm developer. They seemed to go bust faster than we could stay in touch with them, and one was always incorporating another from the Isle of Man or the Channel Islands. We never met the same rep twice, and we lost our confidence. Perhaps it was daft, and maybe I'd be a rich man today if we'd signed on the dotted line, but I was glad when it was over and the subsidies changed. They have to use their own money to build turbines these days, and that has taken the wind out of their sails.

CALVES

June

Our first calves were late, or maybe I did the sums wrong. It takes nine months to make a calf, but the date for their arrival came and went again. I drummed my fingers on the table and began to watch summer sliding past in quiet desperation. It was tempting to fill the delay with worry; I conjured up disasters from a wealth of veterinary advice. I wallowed in horror stories of caesarian sections, then stashed money for the inevitable vet bills and tried not to think about the calves which killed themselves and their mothers in birth.

So the first arrival was almost an anticlimax. I walked round the cattle after a cool, dry morning and found one of the heifers absent. The grass was dry and sparse, and the mud crumbled under my bare feet. I wandered quietly through banks of whin and brambles and found that she had been watching me all along. A calf lay at her feet, curled up like a cat and fast asleep. The birse came up on my head with a prickle.

There had been no sign of labour or impending delivery. The calf might have fallen from the sky, but it was hale and hearty, a little heifer overwhelmed by its first few hours of life. Here was a fresh reminder that these animals scarcely needed me at all, and I realised that all my fears of disaster and complexity were based on commercial cattle – big animals bred for size and bulk. In the pursuit of heavy calves, we have pushed cows to the limits of their capacity, so it's hardly surprising that they now depend upon human midwives. Native breeds can handle the job without much difficulty, and it is unusual to do more than simply let it happen. I stepped quietly away and held the picture of the young heifer in my head. Clear skies, dust and the clattering buzz of craneflies.

We returned the next day with ear tags. Calves have to be tagged soon after their birth, and the chore is a kind of vandalism. Clean, unblemished animals have their ears defaced by neon yellow plastic. But this calf entered the great bureaucratic system of record-keeping with little more than a quiet shudder. Hardwired to hide from predators, she lay flat on the ground with her head stretched out like a fawn. Her mother eyed me warily, and I kept a stick close at hand. New mothers find it easy to flatten and smash the human taggers, and I like my ribs intact.

A second calf has come this evening, not long before sunset. The heifer lies in the shade of the May blossom, doggo in the dusk. We walk towards them and pass through chambers of warm, scented air like rooms in a long corridor. The sun has poured heat into the soil, and now it radiates into our feet. Long rags of afterbirth trail from her tail, and she resents our visit. Mothers know that secrecy pays dividends, and they pull away from the herd in the final hours before birth.

Now there is a galaxy of moths swirling like snow in the thick grass, and the new calf's markings are absurdly clean and white. She is glowing in the blue twilight, and we stand back in silence and let the bats trickle over her. We listen as she stands to suckle her mother's pink teats – a soft click and swallow under the rising moon.

We leave under the cover of darkness, just as the herd gathers to meet this new calf. Mother meets them, and the stillness hangs with curious snuffing. There are not many visitors on this far-flung hill; each new arrival is noteworthy. The beasts convey their interest in a thousand tiny hints and gestures. I begin to see how little of their communication is verbal. Here are flicks and arches, an angled ear and a rolled eye. The flat, droning MOO of children's books is reserved for impatience and salutation. Everything else is expressed in subtleties which heap themselves in deep complexity. Good farmers read the detail; they have a wide-eyed perception of mood and body language, but even the sharpest human eye would have missed much during these gentle, thoughtful moments of welcome.

*

I lay out one morning with the rifle and watched the last pair of curlews over a quarter mile of rough grass. Dawn broke, and I heard the birds wailing in panic through the blue stillness. An old familiar shape was coasting through the misting rushes like a ghoul. It hardly mattered how the birds swooped and screamed; the fox had found his way onto the nest like a pagan sprite.

I sat back from my binoculars. Surely this was some kind of nightmare, an illusion conjured up by that strange blue light between stars and the nodding bobs of cottongrass. I would wake up at any moment and find it was daylight, and I'd shudder at the memory of this eldritch gloom. Things would go back to normal, and the sun would play on safe eggs and happy parents. I wondered whether or not to stalk down into the moss and try a shot at the fox, but I decided against it because it would have been personal, and it would've made no sense.

They say a fox can trot for twenty miles in a night. Kill the local fox and another will soon pop up in his place. I once followed those slim and winding tracks through five miles of snow, and he never paused or broke step in all that time. 'Predator control' only helps when it comes in a sustained, collaborative squeeze across large areas. I'd seen it in Yorkshire and Angus, where farmers work together over many miles of moorland. Curlews are holding their own or even expanding in those places, but anything less than full engagement is almost pointless.

I'm one man against the tide, and I'm the last person still working in this old direction, so I begin to wonder how it would feel to stop trying. There's a tragic irony in the fact that our hill offers some of the best curlew ground you could imagine in June. And it's improving: the cattle stir the moss until it's thick with insects and wildflowers; the oats have begun to stir strange old mechanisms in the fields. But still the chicks are sorely lacking. It's no surprise that the birds run through our fingers like water.

I came in that morning and set the kettle on the stove. Hope had drained out of me, and the depth of my investment pressed into my brain like a steel helmet. I'd made it a mission, and suddenly I saw the scale of the mountain before me. I think that's when I first saw the end for our curlews.

*

Galloway calves are small, and they grow slowly. They're in this for the long run, and their first days are knobbly and weak. But they're keen as mustard and know to rise and suck their mothers without any suggestion or hint. That clever bond of cow and calf sets Galloways apart from many breeds; commercial cattle can be bizarrely dopey and dull by comparison. Many commercial calves need help to find their mother's milk. The further we've strayed from old cattle breeds, the muddier that first connection becomes. I hear that some of the elite cattle can only give birth by caesarian section. Their youngsters are raised by a bucket.

Galloways excel in the early days, but strength in one area means weakness in another. A Galloway makes a great mother, but she has a narrow pelvis and she can't bear a big calf. Cross her with a modern commercial bull and she'll die in the calving. So she's destined to rear a tiny calf, and it works because she's naturally gifted and always does her best.

Now match that skillset with another native breed. White-bred Shorthorn cattle come from northern England. They've got big hips for heavy calves, but the cows often need a hand to bring them up. A Shorthorn carcass will be ready much faster than a Galloway, but you spend more time and labour to get there. It's the age-old trade-off between slow and cheap or fast and dear.

But something very special happens when you cross a white Shorthorn bull with a black Galloway cow. As if by magic, the calves take on the best of both parents. The heifers grow up to be tough mothers with the power to produce financially viable calves from the kind of bulls that would kill a Galloway. And the steers fatten quickly on rough grazing to produce excellent beef. We call these animals Blue Greys because they come in a gorgeous blend of swirling roan, but forget the aesthetics, because these animals are a functional triumph.

You can't breed Blue Greys beyond that first generation cross. It's called hybrid vigour, and the magic wears off on a second rub. They spring from a constant collision between

Galloways and Shorthorns, and there's no such thing as a Blue Grey bull. Even at a time when hill cattle are vanishing, Blue Greys are held to be the most credible native animals in circulation. If modern farmers ever take a step back towards traditional systems, Blue Greys will be their first port of call. Maybe I'll try to breed Blue Greys of my own someday, and maybe I'll reconcile myself to the ugliness of the Shorthorn bulls, which always look like they've been crying through their tiny, pinprick eyes.

The annual sale of Blue Grey cattle takes place in the autumn in Liddesdale at Newcastleton, right on the border with England. I go with my mother every year, and we watch the animals turn around the old wooden ring with its open roof and mouldy benches. I see her face in the churning crowd and know that's where my love of cattle sprang from. That ring's as raw and grit-scored as farming gets, and the cattle send their steam up through the open roof so the ring looks like a volcano when you step outside for a roll.

The mart's always busy, and the buyers speak in a babel of accents from across northern England, Galloway and the Borders. There's Geordies and Jocks jostling for position, hawking and buying beasts which hail from that obscure borderland between two nations. If nothing else, Blue Greys put us in a bigger picture; there's life beyond this short horizon.

*

Our first calves sent me reeling. I thought and talked of nothing else. Paid work went undone, and I reneged on so many deadlines that I lost two good clients. I hardly noticed, and I rushed back outdoors to find thick joy in the tousled hair of infant cattle.

Galloway calves are uniquely charming. Within a week they're bearish and saucy, with a keen sense of fun. Soon they were big enough to chase the dogs, and then they ran behind the quad bike in naughty packs of three and four. I whooped at them and laughed as they overtook me, and I called them tykes and rascals and goaded them to come on and gad some more with their tails flying above them like tram electrics. We'd rollicked round another lap until they'd finally fall away to the safety of their mothers, panting and spent. These were fine games for high summer, but I stalled to wonder how far this delight was self-distraction from my own failed crop.

I'd found a poor escape from thoughts of children; every aspect of this life is founded upon fruitful procreation. I'd sat in the frosts of January and listened to foxes shagging like alleycats, telling myself that I heard something more than functional lust. Our first bull was a grand old fellow, but he was too lame to work and we sold him to the knacker's yard, where they broke him down into dog meat. The irony swirled around me, and so did the creeping awareness that if I were a bull, I wouldn't keep myself. This business is calibrated to output and continuity. I was failing on both counts.

We used to have lots of help on the farm. Friends came down from Glasgow because farming was a jolly novelty. They brought pals and partners, and we could steal something like a social life at busy times when we set up work parties to build fences and stack hay. But gradually there were babies to consider, and people pulled away. Galloway is miles away, and our friends came back as mummies and daddies with sensible cars and day bags. They looked over our shoulders at the clock and didn't have time to spare.

We were free and childless. We couldn't have bought land or cattle if we'd had children, but it's lonely being free when your friends are tied up. Of course we wanted the best for our pals, but that was matched by a sense of ending. They became something new, and we were left behind.

I don't know much about babies, though I'm pretty sure they turn your life upside down. It was kind of our friends to promise that nothing would change for us when they became pregnant, but they had no idea what was coming. Of course things would change, and there's no protocol for softening our kind of failure. And it's bizarre that kids are woven into every thread of our lives when the lack of them is a blunt taboo. I butted my forehead against that silence and tried to crack it open; it wasn't easy in my world where men do the job with a smirk and another pint of black stout.

People congratulated me on my first calves. 'Good job,' they said. I wondered what I'd done to deserve that praise, and I tried to accept it at face value; I'd passed a major milestone. The truth is, the cattle did the work and it was little to do with me. My wife and I sat with the young animals on warm nights and watched them play solemn, elven games. They'd scamper and buck through the twilight; a slalom between half-seen thistles. Now and then a calf would come and stare at us, galloping close on slender legs. We saw ourselves reflected in those blue eyes, and I could hardly ignore the thought that we had calves instead of children – a strange ache in the dusk.

The young beasts grew and became a burden. I welcomed their weight, feeling painfully proud of them in themselves and for all they seemed to represent. I walked through my beasts at dawn and dusk and thought of my own bloodlines twining with theirs beyond the record of history. Their weight had begun to pin me in place and I swelled at the joy of this crippling inheritance, the crump and cud of a thousand ancestors. These beasts are the legacy of countless folk long dead. There are many ways to live on.

*

The time came to replace a rotten gatepost. A little rowan tree was growing out of the old one, and the wood had cracked into flakes. This gatepost was the anchor for a hundred yards of wire, and the fence was falling slack. You could see where the cows had been rubbing on the top line, and the barbs were clogged with clods of fluff. It would not be long before the beasts would gather their skirts and be away. Dykes fall and wood rots; this is the kind of work which comes down through generations. It took an hour to dig the rotten post out by hand. Old Wullie Carson knew how to put in a good fence, and the bottom was almost three feet down, nearly beyond the reach of my fingertips. At last I felt the post give way and then I was able to lever it out with a rope and a steel bar.

The new gatepost is a railway sleeper, eight feet long and black as a peat hagg. There are lots of these sleepers across Galloway, stashed or stolen from the old railway lines. Dr Beeching said it was nonsense to run a train from Carlisle to Stranraer and things would be better if we drove around in lorries and cars. That railway had been our main point of access to the world, but he scratched it off the map. In passing, it left a thin, continuous scar from Dumfries to Portpatrick. Now the cuttings are filled with scrub and we gawp at soaring viaducts as if they came from an ancient civilisation. The only good thing about this closure was a glut of railway sleepers, which we hoard and guard with jealousy. The nettles bristle round them.

We all agree that modern timber is rubbish. It rots because it's not treated properly anymore. Some piece of legislation changed the preservation process because one of the chemicals was said to give you cancer. The new treatment is nowhere near as good, and now the fenceposts go soft and wobbly in the ground like old teeth. You have to buy new ones every ten years at three pounds a go, and your best bet is to swap them with railway sleepers which were treated with tar and bitumen in the 1960s. Canny folk hold on to the old timber, and the gnarly blocks will surely live for generations, steeped in skins of sticky oil and tar. I found a stack of the old sleepers in the back shed when we moved in and earmarked them for use. They're older than I am, and they're replacing posts which were hammered in when I was at university.

I met Sanny on the way home from replacing the gatepost. My trailer was filled with rotten wood and I told him that I'd replaced the new posts with some of the old timber which I found in the shed. He asked what the place is coming to, when we replace new things with old. I joke that the old creosote was poisonous. 'We'll probably all live ten years longer now it's banned.'

He says, 'Aye, and we'll spend those ten years replacing rotten wood.'

It was my father who taught me how to replace and mend the old gateposts. He showed me how to backfill the holes around the wood so that you get a tight fit. You drop the new timber in, then you tip a shovel or two of loose soil around its base. Take a smaller post with a flat end and thump this soil flat – you'll know if you're packing it down hard enough because the ground will boom like a drum. You repeat the process inch by inch until the soil starts to lock tight around the timber. Then you can pause to adjust the post and make sure it's vertical. You work slowly, bit by bit, until the soil has a tight grip.

It's tempting to chuck in stones as you go. Stones make a tight hold when you pack them in, and it's a nice shortcut. I started to do it once and my father pulled me up. Stones are for lazy people. Do it properly with soil and you won't need them. Railway sleepers last a long time, but even they will rot one day and they'll have to be dug up again. It might not be for a century, but some poor bastard is going to have to dig out those stones and it'll be a horrible job.

I was astonished. I'd never given a moment's thought to what might come after my job was done. I hadn't realised that I was redoing a job, and someone else would redo it after me. My post was just the latest in a long line of similar posts which have been occupying this same socket for centuries. I'd moaned at the difficulty of digging up old Wullie's post, but it could have been much harder. He'd passed me a quiet, subtle favour. We're used to thinking of ourselves at the front when we're really in the middle with plenty more to run.

My father saw this place before the trees came and the fields were resown. I leant on his experience because he'd known curlews and Galloways in the days before they fell. He'd farmed many of these fields before me and he could even warn of certain boulders which lurked beneath the grass. Every ripple and rock in Galloway has a name of some small fame; there's Gutcher's Lane to the Brockhole Stane; and the Hingin Bane by the Cuddy's Wame; there's words and words to the far horizon, but you soon lose words if you don't use them. And there's no logic to the ones we keep. Of course we respect old names for mountains and rivers, but I like the tales we tell for smaller things because those are all around us. There's Crummie's Knowe, where the bold dog Crummie went in for a fox and never came out. And that wide tree is called Chick's Brolly because Chick was an old

Clydesdale horse and he'd always stand there when the weather was wet.

But my father is too young to have known heavy horses, and many of those fragments came from a time that he'd never seen. They welled up from the people who came before him, and my father was just carrying them forward. Maybe he'd heard a thousand scraps from his father, and maybe nine hundred of them passed in one ear and out the other. That small tenth was kept for no other reason than because he liked the words or they rang a bell. And you can't extract them by force. You can't say, 'Here's a map, now tell me the things you know about this place, starting in the east and working west.' You have to be with him when he sees the tree or the well-rubbed stone, and the words have to come up by themselves. And you can't prepare for the slippery looseness of that inheritance. It comes in a spatter, half heard above the din of a tractor's engine. It's Chinese whispers without a plan or a backstop. I used to worry that I would break the chain and lose them forever, but now I think that most of these bits are meant to fall and be forgotten. They thicken the soil for new stories.

Ten years after he stopped farming, I asked my father if he still looked over the hedges with a farmer's eye as he drove to work in his office in Castle Douglas. 'If you start, you never stop,' he said.

*

The final calf was very late, but he made our hearts burst with joy. He was perfect from nose to tail, a heavy, gorgeous bull with glossy black hair and a crest of white along his rigg like a Mohican. Riggits are always slightly different, but this fellow was the very picture of perfection to me. His mother was a fine young heifer, and she doted upon him with every strain of devotion. But now that I look back on his early days, I find all kinds of subtle warning. He'd run in panic where the other calves had lain still. He'd stumble in odd places and we never saw him suck. My father shattered the spell by pointing out that the calf was lying with his head downhill. 'A healthy animal doesn't lie like that,' he said. 'That's daft,' I said, uncertainly.

Afternoon came and we couldn't find him. He was lying in deep nettles, utterly hollow and too weak to stand. We realised with horror that he'd not sucked his mother and was quietly starving to death. Clouds of flies rubbed their clammy hands around his eyes and he blinked slowly. The first calves had been up and away without a hand to guide them, and here was a fine lesson in observation. I'd assumed that all would be well, and I hadn't checked.

The cow was brought in to be milked. I'd never reckoned to intervene like this, and she resented our handling. She kicked my father in the guts and bent the old boy double, then she crushed me into a gate and left striped bruises down my legs. Soon we had her bound in a halter, and I watched with astonishment as my father whispered his hand down onto her teats. I was used to seeing this man fluttering soft fingers over a desk or keyboard.

She flickered resistance and rolled her eyes, but she let him at last. He spoke to her quietly and she was calm. Soon we had a pail of thick yellow colostrum, which my father called beestings, although even he couldn't remember why. The fact that she still had this milk in her udders seemed to confirm our suspicion that the calf had never sucked. The beestings went into a glass bottle and we offered him a rubber teat, but his tongue was floppy like an empty sleeve. He rolled his eyes and choked, and hot cream poured down my wrist and into my cuff.

We tried to get him up and sucking from his mother in the next few days. We even poured milk directly into his stomach through a plastic tube, but he failed to respond. He developed other slow ailments which shrank him to skin and bone.

Clegs clustered round us as we worked on the ailing calf. These were long, hot days and the bloodsuckers raised our temperature to boiling point. Flies trod shit over our arms, and the stuffy breeze hummed with the blare of giant horseflies which were thick and heavy like shotgun cartridges. These would often land on the cow's ankles and I'd be caught in the crossfire when she kicked them away. Reeling from the punch of those heavy hooves, I'd land in a soup of cream and shit and want to weep. I lifted the calf up and thumbed his heavy bones, but all he'd do is roll those blue, cloudy eyes and gaze by me as if I wasn't there. I began to wonder if this uninterest was just a symptom of something more serious. He began to suck his own navel, and the habit consumed him.

Perhaps there was something damaged in his brain. The vet came and couldn't help; she'd never seen a calf like this one and proposed trying for another week. Another week came, feeding five times a day. Dawn blurred into dusk and the days rolled together in constant fretful labour. I was flattened by the weight of it. My head was dizzy with exhaustion; I lost my temper over the tiniest details and snapped at everyone. When the calf pulled away for the fifteenth time, I'd pull the teat off the bottle and drink the milk myself. It was warm and thick and there was no reason not to love it.

I shuttled back and forth with those bottles of milk. Familiar fields became dull and fearsome on the endless round, and my thoughts rambled through them in chaos. I was obsessed with the need to keep that calf alive long enough to come through. Everybody said it was time to stop, but I was adamant that something would click into place; something would change and the little boy would come good. I rested my brows on his mother's belly and sent jets of her milk down into a tin pail. Her guts gurgled in the morning dew and she smelled of soft grass and all the things I wanted from this life. The calf lay in a bundle and gazed through me without any expression on his face.

In this condition he would neither live nor die. He made no attempt to rise or change, and my work just kept him alive. I'd seen enough to know that his world was numb and dazed, with only a few vague shapes and urges to drive him. It was surely something in his brain, a bubble or a clot which couldn't come right. Perhaps he'd struggled at birth and lacked oxygen at a crucial moment. It was no kind of life, but he breathed on until his fifteenth day.

I sat for a time with the heavy body and listened to the cow eating hay. She hadn't realised her loss; the truth would soon come to her and then she'd low in misery beneath the stars. Moths flickered in the twilight. I nursed a dull, lurching ache in my chest. The bulk and heft of my own frustrations welled into that calf, and I wept for my children and the shame of my own stubbornness.

I often think of my tears in the dust and the hightailed silhouette of calves playing in the twilight. And the old, dumb hills stand above me; they've seen all this and worse.

*

Then came cool days and time to consider. The good calves were fresh and keen, but I was snared on that single failure. In driving out to look at the cattle one morning, my eye was drawn to a curlew standing in the roadside.

He turned his head and winked at me as I passed him. I'd not seen this bird or his partner for three weeks, and I'd assumed that they'd failed and returned to the coast like all the others. I slowed down and frowned. I had work to do, but I was curious. Clashing the gears into reverse, I backed the rattling pickup along the track for a closer look.

Chicks spilled into the wheel ruts on the track. I was ten feet away as they sprawled in the dust, and I mistook them for balls of grass at first. But then I saw them clambering back into the verge, battling against dewy dock leaves which lolled above them like broadcloth sails. My heart roared at my ears as the adult bird flew up in alarm and then dived over the road in wild distress. He landed on the dyke at shoulder height and screamed like a banshee, calling me to look away and ignore that glimpse of life in the grass. His cries were only half heard. I was utterly drunk on those two youngsters which stood quietly within arm's reach.

Deep, unfathomable eyes blinked quietly; heads down. They'd stopped trying to escape, and now they lay with their thick, staggery legs folded up beneath them, smooth like the colour of river stones. One of them still had an egg-tooth, the little white point at the end of the beak which is used for cracking shells during the hatch. Egg-teeth are lost within a day or two of hatching, so these chicks were freshly minted.

They panted quietly in the grass, burstable and soft like mushy apples. They'd given up trying to run or crouch or conceal themselves. I was looking down on two of the most pathetically defenceless birds I'd ever seen. Did I want to pick them up? They'd allow it. Did I want to bury my teeth in their bodies? They'd gently offer themselves. We all looked at one another as a second curlew came to fly overhead. I assumed it was their mother, and I continued to hold that family in the palm of my hand. That fragility was awful.

At last I moved and the adult birds followed me down the track and over the bridge. I parked in the verge and pulled out a pair of binoculars from the glove box. The river smelled of cool water and meadowsweet, and I watched the parents return to the roadside. I was reeling at this discovery which made me feel small and ignorant in the sunshine. The nest had clearly been in the rushes below the house, so how could I have missed it for thirty days of incubation? And how could the predators have missed it too? We get used to patronising these cunning old birds, and we forget that they can work wonders without our help.

As of that moment, I was hooked on the chicks. Every trip to visit the calves took me past the young birds, so I made a point of pulling over and checking in three times a day. This was safe if I stayed in the pickup and scanned with binoculars, and the adult birds stopped complaining after the first day. They ranged through the deep grass and stood sentinel while their chicks hunted around sprays of orchids and ragged robin, old Wullie's legacy spelled out in a meadow.

Those young curlews were horribly fragile. They ambled through the moss like drunkards, and I could often hear them before I saw them. Their tiny moans ran as constant beneath a clatter of skylarks and I winced to think of how easily they might be found by a fox or a stoat.

The adult birds were fearless to the point of suicide in defending their young. I watched them fly to attack almost every bird and beast which came into view. They flayed a heron and chased a deer across the open ground. The appearance of a crow would send them into a fury and they mauled buzzards with dazzling bravery. The chicks ignored every word of warning and they watched their parents fighting kites as if the outcome would have no bearing on their day.

Young curlews are pathetically naïve. They rely on mixed and choppy country to hide them, and they're doomed without it. It's staggering to imagine how many chicks must be wiped away in their first three or four days in the modern world. And it is heartbreaking that disaster comes after a month of hard work and the cusp of progress. If you're in the business of eating curlew chicks, you just have to pick them up off the ground. The birds used to fare much better in the mixed camouflage of the meadows, but it is still an awful chasm.

HAY

Summer Solstice – the Longest Day

Battering heat and a dry wind to take your breath away. Even the swallows are cowed by it; they pant on the tin roof as their beaks run down their necks in melting shadows.

Broom seeds crackle in the sun, but I can't hear them behind the scream of the grinder as I sharpen the mower bar in the yard. Modern machines cut grass like a lawnmower – a drum whirls cutting blades in tight orbit. My machine is a clipper from the 1970s, and the detachable blades dance back and forth through the grass like a mad crocodile. Sparks blare and soon the teeth are hungrily keen. I will need coarse gloves to refit this bar, otherwise it will start its work on me.

Butterflies cruise over the stones. The bull lies in the shade. It seemed unimaginable in the dire, sodden days of February and March, but now it is dry and he needs me to bring him water. I lug dribbling pails out to his trough and he drinks them in long pulls, a gallon at a time. Streamers of drool blow in the hot breeze. 'Gollup,' then his eyes roll and he bellows through his freshly wettened whistle and the yard rings emptily.

There is no colour in this bright place. The light has burnt colour away and now the blade is just white like the nettles and the stone walls both. The grass has parched on the shallow soil, and the rocky knowes have crumbled back to cracks and powder. Grasshoppers rub their hands with delight; they slitter in the seedheads which flare up like a bow wave at my feet.

The bull's coat has grown woolly and brown like old loft insulation. I feel the sweat in his withers and rub the fine skin of fat which grows over his muscles. He turns his head to lick an itch and the curve of his neck bulges in rippled rows as if it were already bound in butcher's string. His muscles grow; I can't help seeing the cuts of meat through his leather. Clegs cannot resist an early taste. They drive their teeth through his skin and sample the blood as if it were claret.

The oats grow by the hour. Small birds crowd into the rising crop, and the house is suddenly filled with the buzzing whine of a yellowhammer. We have an old name for this garish little bird which stands like a canary along the dyke tops. We call him a yorlin, and he stands below the kitchen window and pastes the place with long, repetitive songs through a shimmer of heat. Yorlins are scarce here since we stopped growing cereal crops and allowed grassland to prevail; a few linger in the fringes, but nothing to what they were. This bird is a small, yellow endorsement of my return to mixed farming, and I cherish him.

It has not taken long for the young oats to grow tall enough to hide linnets and redpolls when they land among them. Now the crop is well rooted, it carries a ripple of wind. Swallows course over the leaves in tight formations of five and ten. They fight and squabble, then winkle out flies which seem to love the warmth of the bare dark soil.

Our neighbours are making silage on the fields below the farm. The tractors shimmer in the heat, and by afternoon the bales are wrapped in shiny black plastic. I wince in the glare and see them beady and tart like elderberries on the yellow field. I stand in my shorts and grind my blades, catching sight of my bare feet on the granite setts below. The sun rasps my back until the skin bubbles like egg white. There is a smell of burning dust, pineappleweed and cut grass.

Soon the heat will fade and the yard will fill with warm, fresh perfume: meadowsweet, bog myrtle and honeysuckle. The swallows will run riot through the doorways in the yard, shuttling bundles of flies to their gaping doom beneath the rafters. Thick twilight will come for an hour or two, and night birds will drone in the shallow darkness. The swallows will fall quiet and bats will crackle like cigarette papers beneath the stars. But for now I am red-faced and livid, working on a job I should have done months ago.

Forgetting the vows I made in winter, I tell myself that I would rather be too cold than too hot.

*

When you start farming from scratch, you lack the simplest things. Forget specialised seed drills and sowing machinery; we didn't even have any string. Some farms have entire sheds filled with rags and clips, pallets and bits of wire; mountains of 'stuff' which fills a gap and allows you to improvise. Most of it has been salvaged from other jobs, and you just pick it up as you go along. But we had nothing.

So we made a list of the things we needed. It ran to three pages and is still running, from jubilee clips and gate hinges to socket joints and syringes. We started to scan through classified listings in the local papers, but the most fertile pickings were found at car-boot sales. We came away with wheelbarrows and coils of good rope, and soon we'd put a winter of hay behind us and could lay our hands on a mile of baler twine. This stuff holds the farm together and covers every emergency. It often holds my trousers up.

So we came to this work without any baggage. We chose Galloways and rough country, and everything else fell into place behind them. For all I mourned a lack of washers and pop rivets, I was keenly aware that starting afresh is a rare privilege in this ancient place. Most of my neighbours inherited something fully formed from their parents. Some found happiness in that continuity, but many wrestled to steer their farms into something different. Lots of farmers never manage to break this loop and pass the land to their children having simply kept it in order for a few decades. I wondered how I would feel to be taking on my father's business, battling his ruts and patterns to find my own direction.

We were free to follow our love, but even so I was starting to find that farming is a steady, draining slog. And I could never ignore the certain truth that I worked beside people who merely tolerated this life. Maybe, like us, they had found pride or pleasure in some part of the work at first, but owning and working land is no automatic joy. There's no escape from undone chores and the smell of shit on your boots. Tiny niggles bug themselves into a torment until the fields are scarred with failure and the farm becomes a black den. And there are some farmers who just hate farming, and they always have. They work the land because they're trapped and they've lost track of the outside world. It looks like resilience, but it's really resignation.

I dwell on the revelation that a local man learned to play the violin in the final months before his suicide. His father had left him the farm, and he'd worked there for almost seventy years as if choice was unthinkable. He'd pressed his music teacher to keep their lessons a secret, and the story only emerged at his wake. We wondered what he'd been grasping for in those final days, who might he have been without that yoke on his shoulders.

It's no small thing to farm in this place. The soil is black and deep, and that exit is always open. I walked beside an old friend as we stepped from the kirk after a suicide ten years ago. I said I couldn't believe the loss, which came after what seemed to have been an up beat and a corner turned. She shrugged and said, 'It happens,' with all the grim, broken-hearted resignation of the hills behind her.

I also work through days of dark moods and sour temper. But I'd have been crushed to feel that emptiness beneath the hum of an office strip light or a dripping tenement close. Pain is a different thing under wide and rushing skies. Even in the bleakest moments of solitude, I draw a selfish glow from that kind of darkness. I hoard the prickle of sleet on my face and endure it, telling myself that nobody else would. I turn away from the warmth of sharing because now I see this place runs far deeper than play or simple sunshine.

*

The time to cut grass grew closer. When I said that I wanted to make hay, people sighed and gave up with me. Silage is the currency now, and the new grasslands were made with that end in mind. It's much easier to preserve soggy grass in black plastic bags than it is to dry it out like herring in the sun. And the climate has changed so much in the space of thirty years that silage has swept hay into the dustbin. You need four consecutive days of good weather to make hay, or three if the conditions are perfect. You just can't bank on that nowadays.

I used to buy whatever silage or hay I could find. I wasn't picky and I didn't have any grass of my own, so I leant towards silage because it's easy and every farm has a bale or two spare to sell. A single round bale would last my heifers for five days, and that freed up my time and made life easy. When

I took the new field on, I was able to harvest my own grass, and I wanted to make hay instead. Modern weather might have made the crop chancy and unreliable, but it's not impossible. I trailed back through old tales of curlews nesting in the hayfields, and the thought made me dizzy enough to find out more.

For all I fretted about those curlews, I was advised to push on with the status quo. People said, 'Stick with silage. Work the good fields hard; it's a waste to take less.' So much labour has gone into improving this ground that the idea of letting it go is close to sin. Gallons of solemn, devout sweat wrestled this place out of the wicked wilderness and made it good. We didn't inherit the work of our ancestors simply to let it wallow and founder. We have the means to reseed and ramp up production, and you'd be mad to do anything else. For all I was taking my work seriously, most people said I was just playing. And I know enough of the real world to understand why I was out on a limb.

Thick, nutritious silage fields can be cut two or three times in a summer. It's great stuff and the cattle do well on it, but the first crop comes off when the birds are still on their nests. Any eggs which have survived the foxes are munched into chaos by the whirring blades. It's hard to spot the nests as you work the fields, and contractors are paid for the amount of work they do so they run as fast as they can. Heavy machines rush through the fields like bulls in a china shop and the wreckage is devastating. You might get three times as much grass from a good commercial silage field, but birds pay a grim cost for it.

Measure that against hay which takes the whole crop in one sweep. You leave the grass until it's grown tall and thatchy and the nesting birds are away. It might have less feed value, but here's fibre and forage for slow fermentation, exactly the kind of fuel you need to power the steady, careful growth of native cattle. Good hay hisses through your fingers like sand and smells like pressed flowers and old books. Beasts and birds both love it, but if you measure success in speed and turnover, hay is lunacy.

The right weather forecast came at last and I was ready to go. My carefully restored mower was a delight and the blades worked keenly through the grass with a click like cutlery. The tall seedheads fell in a wave and the tractor was filled with gales of silky pollen which scoured my eyes and made my nose pour in misery. Docks, buttercups and nettles were slain where they stood, and soon there was a track of dead vegetation lying behind me. The heat shimmered and the greenery faded to a pastel blue.

Progress is slow with an old mower. I worked for five hours on a six-acre field, and I stepped out to unblock a snag every ten minutes. I watched over the fence as my neighbour arrived with a modern drum mower. He cut a field twice the size of my own and left again after less than an hour. He waved and was gone.

I plodded over that field in steady patterns and I scorched myself in the sun like a rotisserie chicken. Soon my arms were red and sore, shiny with motor oil and flock-coated with pollen and grass seed. The black Bakelite steering wheel rubbed my palms into a smeary mess and drips of sweat plopped off my nose. The passage of time was meaningless.

In the last hundred yards before lunchtime, a young hare rose up from beneath my blades and ran away leaving a track in the tall grass. Lots of small animals are killed by grass mowers; the problem is less to do with cutting and more a product of speed. My steady, lumbering progress allowed me to look out for and spy signs of life. It took me so long to make headway that wildlife could move away.

Some animals are naturally programmed to lie still in the face of danger, but I was moving at a slow walking pace with a seven-foot cutting implement and would have been able to see a roe kid or a leveret before the blades chewed it into mince. It's not foolproof, but it's far better than the modern mowers, which are designed to be driven at thirty miles an hour, operating a twenty-foot span of whirling blades. Even in the days when we used to mow hay by hand, we'd still kill the odd curlew chick. You can't throw a sharpened scythe around without expecting some collateral damage, but the problem has been driven into overdrive by the need for speed. I started to cut my field in the assumption that the old ways are too slow. Pondering the idea over several hours of noisy labour, I began to wonder if the new ways are too fast.

*

I once trailed a fox back to his den in a cleft of old stones. This was in a bad piece of awkward hill country, and I found the fresh soil strewn with fragments of the summer's bounty: a grouse wing, some mice and a headless adder lay in the sun. For all he's catty and careful, the fox is often messy at the den, and it's a weakness in him. I walked with my rifle onto the crags to wait for his next move and in walking I found a shred of upturned moss. Cows will sometimes kick through the tumps and leave a mess in their wake, but this shred was more deliberate. It had been turned upside down and the roots were pale and fluffy in the sun. I picked it up and found it was covering a narrow hole and two feet which clawed up towards me. I had discovered the remains of a curlew chick; the bird had been dead for a week. A fox will often hide his food for later, and I found another chick a little further on under another piece of moss. This one was headless. I had a long wait that day and had plenty of time to wonder if the little birds had even tried to hide.

Days passed and our curlews followed their chicks through the rough grass. Haymakers pray for good weather, and so do chicks. The youngsters aren't big enough to control their own body temperature and struggle in the cold. If they start to feel a chill, they rustle into their mother's skirts and recharge. That's fine in short relays, but if it's cold and wet for hours on end they'll spend so long brooding that they'll miss the chance to feed. Then they're on the back foot, and they're more likely to catch a chill to kill them. But we had steady heat, and the little birds were free to roam and hunt for hours at a time. When they were tired, they would just flop down into the grass and nap like puppies. Bad weather kills more young birds than any fox, and a trend towards wetter summers is surely playing a part in the curlew's decline.

If a chick can live to be a week old, it suddenly becomes a more viable prospect. A light comes on and it'll start to shoulder some of the burden of its own care. They begin to heed warnings and contact calls. This new skill makes them wily. And if they can live for two weeks, they'll start to grow feathers and develop some of their own waterproofing.

It wasn't long before our youngsters were sassy and thoughtful, and they pushed far away from their parents. The adult birds stood guard all the while. A crow or a buzzard was acknowledged with a hacking bark; the chicks suddenly knew that that sound meant danger. They could vanish like shadows in the grass; something like magic swallowed them into cover at the slightest twitch of alarm. I could be gazing at a bumbling chick and then suddenly find it utterly absent. The soul and presence of the bird was wholly gone and there was only a clod which looked a bit like a chick. And when danger vanished, the youngsters would come back to life. They'd breathe again and resume their careful striding.

I piled up pages of notes. It has become so rare to find curlew chicks in Galloway that I couldn't afford to miss a single detail. I told Sanny about the chicks and he said, 'Dafties, aren't they?' I said that they were at first, but now they were getting bright and canny.

Sanny had hit a fair few curlew chicks with the big drum mower in the 1990s. He couldn't have known how many because the blades mash up the birds into a fine mist and don't leave much to count. He'd try to avoid them if he could, but there were so many curlews that it was hard to care about every one. Besides, they were dafties and there were always more to come. Nobody had ever cared about wild birds before. If he cut them up by mistake, then the hills were filled with replacements. The world was so big that he could never make a dent in it. What was his damage against a thousand years of continuity?

He came down the road to see the chicks with me in the pickup. They were a hundred yards into the field that afternoon, and we needed the binoculars. Sanny took a while to find them and get focused, but then I heard him whisper, 'Oho, you wee bugger,' and that was him hooked too. He hadn't come across live chicks for a decade, and he'd never really put time into seeing them. I noticed that his van began to appear on the track in the mornings after he'd been to get the papers, just for a quick look, like.

*

The sun batters down and the mown grass wilts like damp paper. I climb up onto higher ground and watch the colours change for half an hour until sunset. The river loops in a curling splay around that field, and I look down on a vee of the open sea. This used to be a playground for smugglers, and I can imagine the dark boats lurking in the tide with loads of brandy and lace from the Isle of Man. People would come up to this vantage point and signal to the boats when the coast was clear, and then the cargoes would bump ashore in the moonlight.

In the last few years of his life, Robert Burns took work in the customs house in Dumfries. It was his job to grapple with the smugglers, and for all he's now the darling of the Scots, he gave us grief in Galloway. Royal Navy ships patrolled the Solway, but it was hard to counter the sheer weight of incoming goods and the general backing that smugglers had in the hearts of Galloway folk. Ever ready to fight the establishment, we reckoned the king had no right to a share of the profits on fine and fancy goods. So there were Dutchmen and pirates on the Solway shore, and they stashed their contraband in a network of caves along the coast. There's one in the woods above the hayfield, and I doubt more than a dozen people know it's there.

My father used to play in that wood when he was a boy, and he told great tales of the smuggler's cave. When I was a boy I went there too. I took a friend from school and we knelt down together and peered into the darkness. The entry had collapsed and was only a foot square. All over the world there are kids pretending to explore smugglers' caves, but we had one for real. And it was horribly, scarily, real.

I don't know what got into me, but I knelt down and grovelled head first into that rooty gap. The first part was short and low, but soon it opened out and I could almost stand up. I had a piece of baler twine tied around my waist and my pal held onto the end of it because that's what cave explorers do. It's hard to imagine what good that twine would've done me if the ceiling had collapsed, but we never thought of that. My father had said that the cave was full of bones and bullion, but the yellow glow of my torch revealed a golf putter and a burst lightbulb. We recovered these riches and tried to reimagine the putter as a musket. By the time we romped home, the trip had been a roaring success. It was disappointing to find that nobody had noticed our absence.

I look again to the sea and down to the creeks where the smugglers ran in the darkness. It is hard to imagine them on a cool, fresh summer's evening. Smuggling is moonlit work.

The hay came good on the following day. I turned the fallen grass after breakfast when the dew had burnt off, and I pulled the whirling hay bob behind me like two massive egg beaters. These machines are meant to fluff up the grass and turn it to catch the sun, but the rows felt sticky and lank at first. Soon there was a breeze which slipped into them, and a climbing sun scorched the rows into a silvery mat. The tractor growled and whisked the grass into a wobbly mass which quivered like down. It was a living thing again, like one of those fortune-telling fish you find in a cracker which tell you if you're fickle or false.

A single dark cloud passed over at midday. It had wandered over the sea from the Isle of Man, and tiny spots of warm rain fell for a minute or two. Even a bald man might've missed it, but the whole field was utterly transformed by this shift in atmospheric moisture. The fortune-telling fish was dead. Floss became lank again and the shiny strands were gummy and dull. It was hard to pinpoint what the change had been, but it was astonishing. Just as magically, the sun returned and the field was restored to its glory in less than half an hour. I sat in the freshly dried crop and ate my lunch, wondering if the grass around me resented my sweat.

Dew came again in the evening and the crop was bogged with it. The hay seemed to die again. Tiny beads of moisture formed like mould on its corpse. This dew was a temporary setback, and the next sun would pick up the job where the last had left it. Birds called across the merse, and the world smelled dry and clean. The landscape grumbled with a hum of machinery far into the small hours because the big silage contractors don't care about dew; they just need the grass gathered in time for the next job.

Cut fields are the best place to find a fox. He comes threading out from the brambles to hunt for scraps of mower meat. There's a damp charcuterie of shredded mapsies and pipit chicks waiting for him. That's no problem to me, but there are curlew chicks around here too. The idle scrounger soon becomes a hunter, and I wait in the gloom with my torch and rifle. It hardly matters which way the wind's blowing because now I smell more like grass than human being. I squeak my lips and the hunter rushes down the torchlight beam to see if I am a man or a mouse.

*

I needed lots of help in my first year of haymaking. The work calls for a fine blend of art and science, and it's easily botched by an amateur. It's not hard to dry grass, but hay is made when it becomes a bale. That final step relies on some of the most complex and mercurial machines ever designed by pre-digital man. I was lucky that a neighbour offered to bring a baler over and bind my first crop into small, manageable parcels. I wouldn't have known where to start on my own.

Balers occupy a rare and vaunted position in local folklore. Baling is a privilege that can't be wasted on boys, and I was a bystander in that first year. I made a big effort to hide my excitement and delight as the huge machine pulled into the hayfield and started to unfold out of 'transport mode'. It came as a grand piano, but soon it was a barrel organ, complete with crank handles and a set of puffing flues. All we needed to complete the scene was a man with a neckerchief and a monkey.

I stood well back, but I saw everything. Fingered drums gather up the grass and pass it to a chute where it's chewed and pounded to cubic flakes (and that's where the whumping din comes in). Then the flakes are punched and shot with thick iron needles which tow lines of twine in complex binding patterns. Finicky fingers tie that twine and then cut it using a delicate, gorgeous mechanism that would baffle an owl. At full stretch, the metal chassis is alive with twitching levers, crackling chains and whirring pulleys, a mechanical organism guzzling grease and farting gales of dust.

Here is a piece of machinery to be reckoned with – faded yellow lettering proclaimed it to be a 'Hayliner', nine feet wide, eighteen feet long and weighing well over a ton. The baler was old enough to be fragile and vast enough to be lethal. I was glad that I'd been relegated to the sidelines, and I followed on behind to roll the bales and start the stack.

In my second year, I was allowed to drive the baler under strict supervision. I felt the shuddering lurch of responsibility as it lumbered over the dry ground and gathered up the crop. Sanny sat on the mudguard and tutted, lighting small fires with the cinders of his fag. If I slowed down he would yell, 'Gie her some bloody welly, boy. Jeeesus!' In Sanny's world, everything was a feminine noun, from the weather (she's grand) to the wheelbarrow (she's fucked). When conversation ebbed, Sanny would suck his teeth and baffle me with 'Aye, she's the boy.'

Cubular bales jerked out of the tail and fell with a dunt on the yellow field. Friends had come to watch and help; they tossed the bales to the sides of the field and loaded them into a trailer, marvelling at the weight of them. These were as light and flossy as pillows, but the work was hard and slow as they were piled up in batches of sixty. It was almost dark by the time we finished. Sanny had commandeered the baler and another friend arrived with a crate of beer. Swallows rushed through a stench of diesel, dried flowers and sweat.

Haymaking is a kind of sublimation. Grass becomes hay with little more than a rub of sunshine. I was considerably younger than every piece of machinery we'd used in this job, but the work had made it something new. I looked at the machines where they lay in the dusk and knew them as living things. The reaper had a hank of dead nettles trailing from its teeth like a strand of half-chewed sinew. The bob was dizzy and sore, and the moving parts were bound in greasy scabs of grass which came away when you picked at them. Nobody could deny that the baler was the star of the show; the stylish compère, with a joke and a wink for everyone. The barrel organ had played its simple rhythm in dust and pollen, and now the evening seemed empty without it. I'd done three days' work in an afternoon. Blood dribbled out of my blisters and I could have wept for joy.

I carted the hay home in high trailers which scraped the evening trees and left a swirling wake of grass on the road. My wife sat by my side, and we worked on as the bats came up to scuttle in the dusk. A stack grew in the shed, and we built them in a pattern that Sanny showed us so the bales would lock together and stay tight. It was long after our bedtime, but the work overruled silly routines because the rain was coming and the moment was ripe. By the time we fell onto that mattress, we were wholly done and triumphant. The smell of hay rang from our clothes and the gap of the open window.

Then rain came after long dry weeks. The soil sucked it up, and the surplus rolled down over the hard ground into the river. But our grass was safe under a tin roof, and we'd cheated the weather. The smell of dry flowers chimed with the scent of rain on hot soil. We went to sit in the shelter of our stack and watched the water falling in sheets from the tin roof and the chuckling gutter. We laughed and rolled about like kids, and then Sanny came and we pulled ourselves together. He said we'd done alright. That was glowing praise.

And the rain kept falling. I recovered my waterproof trousers from the cupboard and unrolled the legs. They were crispy and hollow like an old cocoon, and I rediscovered smells which had been locked up since winter. There was cow shit and silage to remind me of a time before all this daylight. Droplets gathered on the cattle until even the blackest animals were cast in a silver foil of dew. The calves had never known water like it, and they tossed their heads and ran through starry galaxies of yellow bog asphodel. Young swallows lined out along the fences and squalled to be fed, but their parents were already looking ahead to breed again.

Then the oats began to ripen, and smears of gold began to sway in the green sea. I pinched the fattening seeds and found them soft and soggy. Milk bled between my fingernails with a chalky tang of starch. A wet wind rode through the dangling heads with a rattling whisper. I walked quietly around the margins to see weeds which had risen as if from nowhere.

With the help of a book, I managed to identify dead nettle and fat hen, shepherd's purse and sun spurge. These are common enough, but I'd never seen them before. They belong in an arable world, but the small birds and feisty beetles remembered them like old friends. Maybe the seeds had lain dormant in the soil since this field was last worked, and I felt a rush of excitement at the idea of stirring old Wullie's world back into life.

I tried to picture a time when every farm was built on fields like these, with ladybirds and spiders tumbling like sailors through the masts and rigging. How easy it must've been for curlews and all manner of wild birds when the world was overflowing with variety. Our beasts peered over the dyke and eyeballed the oats. They stretched their long blue tongues to gather some scent or flavour from the nodding heads, and I narrowed my eyes and smiled at their living mass of black and white in a wide pool of green and blue.

But for all this deep and stirring joy, I'd begun to see why folk don't keep cattle in the hills anymore. It's hard and friendless work, and it goes against the grain. There's little reward beyond the love of cattle; this life would be a dire cage without that. I heard a word of advice in the days when I was dithering about whether or not to start with Galloways. A farmer from Wigtown said, 'Go with the cattle you love; you'll never make much money and you'll have to work with them every day for the rest of your life. You won't stand a chance without love.'

We rediscovered our loneliness in the days after Beltane. We'd go for weeks without seeing anyone of our own age, and some days crawled by in absolute isolation.

I took a course for young farmers on grass production at the agricultural college and hoped to broaden my horizons and make some farming friends.

My classmates seemed to come from a different world; their conversations were noisy and hard to grasp. They spoke of grass in tons per acre and asked questions about Tissue Deposition and Live Weight Gains. Their industry was shiny and new, decorated with gadgets and technology. I asked about birds and the lecturer frowned and said, 'This is an agricultural course.' My classmates had never heard of curlews.

I came away feeling even more isolated, but it was some consolation to realise that my work was no better or worse than modern agriculture. The boys (because they were all boys) dealt in GPS systems and ultrasound scanners which tell if your cows are pregnant. But I was learning to tell which cow was pregnant by the shift and weight of her walk. They spoke of technology which was measured in megabytes and download speeds, but mine depended upon spanners and rivet hammers. Both are easy when you know how. There was no love for hill cattle on that course.

I might as well have been pushing for Clydesdale horses and steam engines.

BULL

July

Gnats churn like smoke above the oats, and they mingle with drifting seeds and tall streamers of gossamer. The air is thick with business, and I am glad of the hairs in my nose as I work. Regiments of flying beetles fall on my back; some of their outriders drown in my coffee. Then ants come and scuttle on the stones below the hayshed until the black grains of granite begin to tingle and throb.

Swallows course through this soup and skim their bellies over the trailing heads of my oats; living is easy on a day like this. They dash and squabble through the yard in noisy gangs of ten and twenty. There is no way that I can claim the credit for this explosion of life, but I cannot ignore the fact that it seems to centre upon my crop. It was right to pull the turf off that field and take a look inside. Perhaps I have provided a point of focus, but this glut has a root in slow and steady farming, cradled and passed between generations. It has gone from many places and it is only here because we have not spoiled it yet.

The first curlew chick died last Tuesday morning, just after dawn. I looked up from my office window and saw the adult birds diving and wailing in the deep meadow below the house. I had hoped that the chicks would be wily enough to fend for themselves, and I had been pleased to see them hunting for beetles in the grass where the cattle stood. They had been late to hatch, but the summer suited them and the birds grew well on a steady, rolling diet of insects and spiders. The world was their oyster, and I hoped that I might finally see them fledge.

The fox waited until the little birds were juicy and plump, then he quickened upon them like a knife. I know this hunter well; we have been locked in a duel for weeks. His face has become a narrow, sinister vee in the long grass, eyes like buttercups in the twilight. He is now far removed from the glossy luxury of midwinter. He has grown scant and jointy, with a brush like a bunch of rushes. I waited for him that night with a rifle, but he did not come.

The living chick walks on through a drift of buttercups. It does not seem to recognise the weight of expectation which lies upon it. I stop and watch the bird picking through a swarm of small insects, growing apace and beginning to show the start of wing feathers. We drive by after lunch as we go to bring in the peat.

Most of this stuff was cut in May when the moss was rustling with craneflies and grouse chicks scrabbled through the white cotton bobs like bees. The dark, fudgy mud came out of the ground like cheese, and my wife caught the slabs from my spade and tossed them up over the hagg's lip where they lay on the heather like trays of brownie.

Now the blocks are black and crisping in the sun. We have turned them twice in the last eight weeks and they have shrivelled at their corners. Peat needs the wind to dry, and the breeze has licked their skins into a web of blue cracks which run like crazy paving along the flat surfaces. A kestrel has been peeling mice on the little stacks, and shit shows where the grouse have lain in the lee of our piles.

We used to cut a winter's fuel from this peat, but now we only take a few barrows of the stuff. Scientists fret that we're leaking out greenhouse gases, and people tut when I talk of peat smoke. Highland crofters burn peat as part of their culture, but we have no excuse because most of us stopped digging here in the 1990s. We are told that peat should be swaddled and safeguarded, so now our yearly haul has been reduced to a small measure, taken as an act of remembrance.

There is a something valuable in the digging and the slow, drying pull of the wind. I mark the darkest days of winter by burning the summer's peat. It's a symbolic moment to match the flakes of summer hay which I dish out to stands of cold cattle. The peat smoke is chokingly fresh and floral. The scent hangs in the yard beneath the stars and the fire leaves a red cake of ash in the stove. It's a welcome break from cords of ash or pine or the belching stench of heating oil, which is fine to burn.

Sacks of black peat come rumbling off the moss, and I stack them in the yard. I see the curlew chick one more time in the dusk.

I see the curlew chick one more time in the dusk. I will never see it again. I try to picture a sudden, unknowing death in that half-lit fairyland of gossamer and dew. Perhaps it was not a bad way to go, with a broad sky above you and the sound of larks.

*

1914 was the year that a famous Galloway cow called Alexa of Castle Milk won at the Highland Show. The crowds gathered in the bandstands to dodge the clattering rain which hammered down for the full three days of stock judging and events. I've seen a picture of Alexa that day, and she is beyond gorgeous. Two men stand beside her, one in a broad flat cap and the other in a silky topper. It would be the last Highland show for five years.

A month later, the granite men of Dalbeattie became F Company, 1/5th Battalion King's Own Scottish Borderers. On a warm afternoon in August, they formed up at the drill hall in the town and marched to the train. Folk gathered round to watch them go, and every man wore a black grouse tail in the peak of his bonnet. The train huffed them away over the moors, and the town fell to quiet speculation. People hung around the noticeboards at the grocers and waited for news.

The men trained for weeks at Stirling and North Queensferry, and they helped to save Edinburgh from a submarine attack. One of them spotted a periscope sliding through the Firth of Forth, and the full battalion opened fire on it. They were joined by heavy artillery; the Forth thundered with high explosives. But the periscope turned out to be an empty whisky bottle and a reminder that those men had never seen a submarine before.

They'd never heard of Gallipoli either. Most of them had never left Scotland, but soon they'd be dying in the hot rocks of Turkey. More died of dysentery than shrapnel in the endless reek of rotting horses, and the survivors were hard pressed in the Mediterranean sun. There are a few photographs of them in the museum. They're wearing old-fashioned sun helmets, and some of them are trying to smile. Not even the hardest men saw that misery coming. Galloway would never be the same again.

One of the officers commanding 1/5th Battalion was a Captain George Scott-Elliot. He was too old to be called up, but he volunteered anyway and fought in Egypt, the Middle East and France. He'd been an academic and a botanist before the war, and he'd worked hard to bring progress to Galloway.

Speaking to a local audience in 1912, he complained of the wasted land in southern Scotland. He said, 'Many of us have wandered over the moors of our uplands and can bear me out in saying that it is only when one ascends to haunts of the whaup, grouse and blackcock that one realises how great is the amount of undeveloped land in southern Scotland.' His answer was to plant the hills with trees, and the idea got some good traction at the time. There was an appetite for progress and advancement, but real change was just a pipe dream. The hills were so vast and awkward that planting was impossible.

Then the war whittled us down to the last matchstick. Cries went up to find a fresh supply of timber, and the Forestry Commission was established to buy up land and get new trees planted. The government bought 300 square miles of Galloway, and most of this was earmarked for planting. Sheep still grazed that land in the early days, and the shepherds reckoned that nothing would come of the plans. The job was just too big.

Those early days were a matter of trial and error. Nobody had ever done anything like it before, and special kit had to be designed and tested for the work. After a few false starts, the trees began to bristle through in thick oceans during the 1950s. We'd been longing for this chance for a millennium, and suddenly it was lying at our feet. Thousands of acres were consumed by the steady, putt-putt-putt of tracks and chains. George Scott-Elliot would've been impressed, but maybe even he might have winced at the scope of this new power.

It's telling that curlews were mentioned by name in those early calls for change. The old whaups seemed to represent a kind of slackness which could no longer be tolerated. The foresters were told to follow the sound of curlews and to plant their trees on the waste where the birds were striding.

Curlews were wiped from the hills in a single generation, then the Second World War came and made us paranoid about food and drove the curlews out of our lowlands too. The Celts fought the Romans and the Levellers raged at the coming of cattle three centuries ago, but the new forests and farms were just a fresh take on the same old process which has been smouldering for a thousand years. The only difference is that our ancient desire for change has finally coincided with the capacity to make it happen.

It's hard to pinpoint why the loss of curlews should be such a point of regret, and I worry that I'm being nagged by nostalgia again. If I whine about the loss of curlews, people say I should get real and grow up. I try, but I'm hung up on the idea that this loss is telling us about something bigger than birds. Curlews stood for an ancient slackness; they were bound to the old ways, even down to those birds which came back to Wullie Carson. We drew them into us with a steady, hard-won roll of patience and labour which ran for generations, and now their death feels like a death in ourselves.

As for our curlews, they were gone for the year, and that was that. The adult birds saw no point in staying to mourn their stolen chicks, and we didn't hear them again. Most of them will come back again next year, but it's hard to see how the balance will shift. Maybe I'll be doing more and better by then. I don't think I'll ever give up, but I'm still just a fading flare of optimism in a broad sea of change.

I once saw a chick make it to adulthood. I know the early days of this process in explicit detail: courtship, display and nest-building, but the later stages are a novelty because they hardly ever happen anymore. The youngster bounced and fluttered until she learned to grip the air beneath her feathers, then she flew in short, lurching bounds through the rushes.

She smashed through that fine rigging of cobwebs which hangs at knee height on ground like this, then she repaired to a rock where she stood and panted with her shoulders hunched.

I saw her fly a hundred yards a few days later, and then she flew out of sight. The young curlew lingered for a day or two with an adult to keep an eye on her, then the family was gone. Mission accomplished. But one recruit cannot replace the steady loss of many. There will soon come a time when curlews will not return here. Years of steady erosion will see them off.

Old curlews are often disfigured or injured by extended periods at sea or on the hill. Toes become clustered with bunions, and toenails fall off as leg bones warp and buckle. It's hard to explain many of these injuries, but they seem to be more pronounced with age. The implication is that a curlew's death is not a single event but an ongoing process which begins slowly, piece by piece, from the toes up. Death ends slowly too, and shadows linger on the hill beneath the stars.

*

Sanny said the word 'bull' as if it rhymed with 'gull' or 'dull'. He doesn't blink at my own pronunciation, which comes out flat and slow like an Englishman's 'boule'. He says there is 'nocht finer than a geed gallowa bull', and the words sound right in my head, even if I can't say them.

Maybe I lean too heavily on our bull, but he leans heavily on me. They say that a bull is half your herd, and a decent bull can make or break a business. My bull is a champion beyond question because he's mine, and every wrinkle and stamp belongs to me. I'd take his side against any beast in the country.

Riggit bulls are hard to find. Good beasts are spread so thinly across the country that the pickings are slim. Some of the best animals come from Devon and Cornwall, but that's

400 miles away and they struggle with TB in the West Country. Even with the cleanest bill of health, it's hard to stomach the risk.

In the old days, bulls were lent and borrowed between small farms and crofts. The animals were readily shared, and only wealthy farmers had their own. Nowadays there are disease concerns and health schemes which make it hard to balance the bother of moving cattle between different herds. Lending is all but dead, though there are modern ways to share. I could have bought straws of semen so that my heifers could be artificially inseminated; that industry is dominated by big cattle and commercial interests. Riggit straws are hard to find, and even if you can pin them down there is very little choice.

I did my sums and realised how hard it would be to justify the expense of buying and keeping my own bull. Most farmers reckon that it's only worthwhile when you have more than fifteen or twenty cows. I only had seven at the time, and I had to balance the advantages against a heavy toll of cost and inconvenience. He'd have to be kept separate from his harem for nine months of the year. That alone would call for more space and a rehash of my indoor arrangements. And I'd need extra feeding and another animal to keep him company. Bulls pine in solitude and can go mad without a pal. Problems hang around them like a swarm of flies.

There were many good reasons to duck out of buying a bull, but I couldn't get past the idea of it. Something in me craved the power and heft of a heavy beast. I wanted a bull to scare the cushiness of my cows. I wanted him to give me a decent rattling too. My grandfather was never scared of bulls, and I had something to prove. It was time for a bigger challenge and the tang of fresh danger.

It took a year, but I found the boy for us. He had superb parentage and bloodlines which harked back to some of the riggit animals which formally founded the breed in the 1980s. I was stunned by photographs of his grandparents; I had watched his father win the champion's rosette at the Dumfries Show. There weren't many riggit Galloways on the day, but Finlay was a sight to behold. He seemed to represent Galloways as I'd seen them in history books: heavy, round and confident. Modern Galloways have expanded into tall, rangy animals which are clipped to look square and blocky. Finlay was a gorgeous, short-legged oval with good flesh in all the right places. His son was born the following April to a well-established cow with some fine blood of her own.

And he filled our hands. Once the novelty of a new place wore off, he became bold and saucy. Even in his smallness he would shove and buck like a brat. The heifers were soft and gentle, and here was the other side of the same personality. He held me at arm's length, and I carried a stick.

There was a time when I hated him. My bones chilled at the sound of his adolescent moaning. But then he began to mellow. We built some connection, and I steadily learned to manage his power until we could work together in something like unity. Now he's soft and pliable like a half-ton bear. He's devoted to my wife, and if I'm struggling to impress some meaning or guidance onto his day, the merest word from her brings instant obedience.

Time spools by, and I thumb through memories of that early misery and find it's woven itself into this place alongside thick veins of pleasure and fun. I see sunlight on the thorn trees and remember them dark and wet that day he dashed me into the ground. Twilight passes onto the hills and the smell of sodden moss recalls a clash in the gathering pens. This business snags on every boulder, hedge and tree like hair on a bent wire. Now I look from my window across open country and feel a lurch of pride in that grand, heavy beast and the place we share.

It's helpful when friends come down from Glasgow and see him. They're afraid of him and tiptoe around his lumbering bulk as if he were a dragon. Bulls are scary, but I know him so completely that I can measure the risk. They think I'm brave, but really it's knowledge and know-how. So now I think my grandfather's courage was just deep familiarity. We think nothing of coasting around in cars at sixty miles per hour when by rights we should be terrified. But we're used to it. And that's how I began to find my own kind of manliness.

The bull goes out to the hill in July. We feel his absence around the yard and the kitchen window where he loved to lie. The cows wait for him beneath high, dark clouds and he runs to them like a rumble of thunder. Their peace is smashed in the foam of his excitement; he thrashes his head against fallen boughs and tears up the turf in streaks. The cows are appalled and the calves run from him in terror.

Our lad becomes a tyrant. He curls his nose and snuffs at them like a leering pervert. They piss and he licks it in streams, drolling it across his blue tongue and blaring the whites of his eyes. He throws himself around the herd, but injury could undo that strength in a heartbeat. He could easily crack a leg or bust a hip. Some unfixable injury could bring him crashing down and end his career with a bullet in his skull. A working bull is a champion who dances with death; his wretched pride is a rolling dice.

The cows come in season for twelve hours every twenty-one days, and he reads them like a book. He works out a steady rhythm, and every jump is preceded by grunts and moans; here's a way to produce calves – a glorious, hot-bedded crucible where magic can happen. It's grotesque, but I'm glad that we did not choose to buy in straws of semen. A specialist with a shoulder-length glove would have stripped the soul and mystery from this wild festival of lust. I cheer him on from a safe distance.

*

Then our treatments began in the tall, concrete hospital. We turned our backs on the rampant bull and submitted ourselves to sampling. Our appointments were early in the morning, so we had to stay over in the city. I used to have the knack of sleeping in the orange glow of streetlights, but I'd lost it during ten years in the darkness of Galloway. I lay awake and listened to people walking up and down the street outside, wondering why they weren't asleep.

We arrived early, and the nurses let us go by mid morning. Then we met up with friends and went for lunch in the city, and I realised how quiet our lives had become. People rushed by me and I fought the instinct to say 'hello' to everyone. That's what you do in Dalbeattie: you make eye contact and smile, even if you don't know the person.

But the most striking thing was the smell of people. I don't mean dirty bodies or unwashed clothes, but the opposite; a roaring fug of aftershave and fabric conditioner swirled in the wake of every passing body. We got a lift in a taxi and I gagged on the reek of air fresheners hanging from the rear-view mirror. After months in a subtle breeze, I was bowled over by the weight of it. The hills were honing me to find richness in a glance of sunlight or a distant snatch of birdsong. Here was an overload; my nose was being sand-blasted.

We wanted a treat, so we walked to a restaurant in George Square. I felt loud and noisy, and I ordered up heavy jugs of IPA. You aren't supposed to drink during fertility treatment because it harms your success rate. Nobody seems to care that drink makes more babies every year than IVF ever will, and barring us from it felt like yet another petty theft. Besides, I was more ready for a drink after an hour in hospital than I ever was after a day's mowing hay.

What better than a steak, and I was glad to see the menu boasting of Scottish beef. Rib-eyes with chips and grand onion rings like battered bangles. The waitress asked, what sauce did I want? There was Diane or peppercorn – strong flavours to smother your tongue and mask subtle quirks of fat and fibre. I joked and said it wouldn't need a sauce if it was a decent steak. She said everybody has a sauce, and please would I pick.

The plates arrived and the steaks were as big as the sole of my shoe. It would have taken one hell of a beast to produce a rib-eye that size. I realised that 'Scottish beef' is merely a brand to mark down recent provenance. There's a nudge to imply that you're eating some windswept Highlander, but in all likelihood your steak has come from a crossed commercial breed which has finished its final few months on a high-octane ration inside a shed. That meat's perfectly adequate for what it is, but I was spoilt and was hoping for something more.

So the food was fine. Not good or bad, just a shrug on a plate. I'd hate to be the kind of snob who whines over tiny points of pedantry, so I said it was 'Great, thanks' when the waitress came back and asked how we were getting on. But I couldn't find much to praise beyond the rasp of the dark griddle crust. I sawed the steak apart to reveal coarse grains and a washy pink colour. There was no sign of the dark richness and creamy marbling which defines well-matured beef from old native breeds. This animal had put on weight quickly, grown like a nettle and been killed. No wonder it needed a sauce to add some flavour.

After four years with cattle, I began to face the prospect of killing the animals I'd raised from infancy. I recoiled from the thought. I had some connection with every beast, and while some were treasured pals, even the most distant and wary had quirks and charm. I actively disliked two of the steers from our first year. They were ham-fisted and dim, but even they were precious because they bore something of their parents. As the time came to think of killing, I braced myself to do it on a single condition – that the meat should be valued and treasured as a rare and precious thing.

So I'd elevated beef beyond any rational reason and saw it as an extreme treat, the luxurious fruit of someone's long, hard labour. But that's not how modern systems deliver meat, which is an everyday fact of life, eaten at every meal and often from multiple sources without a second thought. The public needs affordable meat and commercial systems provide it. Modern farmers are formidable and adaptable folk working a hard job in a tough climate. If I criticise continental animals, it's only because I'm confident that I can do them no harm. Commercial beef is big business, and projects like mine are less than an eddy in a flood. But I've heard Galloways being sidelined so often that I think they deserve a reply.

If you work with native breeds, you know the drawbacks. The beasts are small and take years to mature, but there are redeeming features. People have taste-tested different kinds of beef. Even with blindfolds, traditional, slow-grown meat comes up on top every time, particularly when it comes from older animals. That's not to say that native beef is essentially better than commercially produced meat, but it does imply that it's different. So try Galloway beef and compare it with a Highlander or a Shorthorn. Then compare your favourite with a continental breed. You'll find they're all quite different.

And it's frustrating how bad we are at celebrating diversity in our meat. It's odd because beef is a premium product, and we like to place value on detail and nuance. Select a medium-bodied Pinot Noir from the Loire Valley and savour notes of cherry and spiced plums, supported by ripe, juicy tannins. Calling it 'French wine' would hardly do it justice, but pour a glass and enjoy it with your 'Scottish beef'.

*

Fergus was tall and strong in his day. Born and raised to farming in Galloway, he grew to be a smiling, gentle giant at six foot six in height. Travelling with friends to the bull sales at Perth, Fergus found his way to see some Highland Games. We don't have Games in Galloway, and the events felt foreign. It's another country up there, but Fergus had a go at flinging a steel ball and ended up smashing their records. The kilties were stunned by that quiet, smiling superman from the far south.

By sixty years old, Fergus was bow-backed and slow. He seemed ancient to me at twelve or thirteen, but we had much in common. Fergus knew all about wildlife, and he dug ponds and planted hedges as if he'd live forever. We held serious conversations about eels and lapwings and the way a sparrowhawk always comes back to his kill.

My father had worked for Fergus in the old days, and they were pals. Fergus had a shallow pond on the back of his hill, and the two men used to sit out there and shoot ducks together. The water was plied with mouldy barley to draw in the ducks, and the birds would rush in to feed when darkness fell. I was old enough to join them when I was fifteen, and I stood with them at the back of the dark whins and watched the night come without any idea of what might happen.

The moon rose and spilled across the sea from Westmoreland and the Lake District. I was trembling with excitement, and darkness brought a gale of wildfowl into our laps. There were massed ranks of wigeon and teal, proud little ducks tumbling in from the stars. Gorgeous, slender-necked pintail joined them, and the cold air hummed with mallard and snipe.

We shot them early and finished after half an hour. Fergus had a labrador called Murdo, and the big dog smashed through the ice to pick fallen birds. I could hear Murdo puffing through his nose in the water, and the white-bellied ducks shone in the moonlight. I had three wigeon and my father had one. Slush sloughed from their dead bellies and chilled my hands to agony, but wild horses could not have dragged those birds away from me. We took four brace for the pot, no more than we could comfortably use. Fergus loved a brace of fat wigeon and used to say that the sound of rushing wings made his mouth water. Sure enough, the little birds are rich and hellish tasty.

I returned the following year in a state of ecstasy. If anything, this night was better than the first. I clung to every tiny detail: the whoop of wigeon above the red, fuzzy glow of my father's cigarette, quiet conversations in the half-darkness, then the bleep of a cock teal under the moon. It didn't take long for those nights to sink a deep root into my brain. I tried to imagine the agony of missing one. I would be inconsolable; surely the year would grind to a halt. Time moved so slowly that next winter might as well be never.

Fergus was so casual about it all. He'd forget to invite us, then he'd come round with an hour to spare and ask if we were free. He loved the sport, but it was just the backdrop to an evening with friends. I could hardly fathom that gentle indifference, and I began to memorise every detail of those nights with rising panic as if every year was the last. I felt and heard everything with desperate intensity.

Then Fergus was ill for a long time. It got to the point where he'd invite us to shoot, but he'd stay indoors by the fire. When the flight was over, we'd walk down to join him in the kitchen for soup and rolls, and he'd smile at our adventures. On bright, moonlit nights, the flight is unending. The duck are restless and they shuffle between ponds until dawn. Fergus read my enthusiasm and sent me back up to the pond again on my own once we'd eaten. There was one time when I stayed on the hill until two in the morning, mumbling with hypothermia and drunk on every detail of the darkness. My bicycle had frozen into the brambles by the time I headed home, but I had four teal to tie on the frame's crossbar.

The colour went from Fergus's face and he died. I soon lost touch with that place, the high hill pond surrounded by thorns and prickles. From where I sit, I could be there in five minutes, but I never go. The idea of that place reminds me of wild joy and the thrill of rushing fowl, and now I realise how I'd spoil that joy by trying to make it last forever.

*

Soon it would be time to mow the oats and begin the harvest. I drove the tractor into town to fill the tank with fuel. It's three miles, but the trip was slow and ponderous, and I made time to trail my hands in the hedges. Coming round a final corner towards the first houses, the tractor stumbled into silence. I'd run out of diesel.

Of course I was an idiot for letting the tank run low, but the real problem was a leak in the fuel return pipe. I'd have to walk into town with a jerrycan, and I'd have to repair the leak before I bled the system to clear out the airlock. This would've been unimaginably difficult a few years ago, but now I can take it in my stride. I plodded towards the town and found a friend in the street. We chatted for a while as the sun began to sink, then I wandered back to find some new hose to replace the perished pipe.

Time ran away with me. An hour passed, but I was enjoying this little job. I hadn't planned to be in this position, and I only had myself to blame. I let myself off with a shrug and wondered how angry I'd have been if this obstacle had come in the days before I knew about machines and cattle. I'd have raged and sworn fit to burst, but the irony is that I like jobs like these. There's satisfaction in doing them well, and I'd have been angry simply because my plans were in chaos. But now I know that plans change and things move. Sometimes it's all you can do to stand still, so take the day as it comes.

It was almost dark when I finished bleeding the fuel injection system. The day had slowly ebbed over an hour, and I drove the lightless machine back into the yard. Birds rushed overhead, and night grew over the moss like an old bruise. The tractor roared in the shed, and then I pulled the STOP lever and silence fell. There are always chores to do before night, and I milled quietly around the yard with buckets and string. The bull belched on the old granite stones.

I came at last to the back door and I kicked off my boots. My wife was away, and I sneaked into my home like a thief. I reached for the light switch, then realised how unwelcome that 'click' would be. The day had spooled out; it was over. I should take the hint and accept the darkness.

I used the glow of the stove to find matches, then I hunted for a candle. The dogs were fed, and I sat for a while with a slab of cheese and watched the flame play shadows over the kitchen. I was being put to bed, and it was easy to hand over responsibility for my day. There was work to do in the office, but I realised that I'd missed my chance to do it. There would be time tomorrow.

And my eyelids were heavy. It's so easy to ignore the natural signs of evening. I wallowed in the last blue hum of day and tried to imagine streetlights flickering on in the town beyond the hill. The setting sun doesn't count for much there – councillors decide how long the day should last.

Low, fluttering light conspired to flatten me where I sat. My book fell upturned on my lap, and I was soon in bed with the windows wide open like cupped hands to catch the night sounds. Cattle moving and birds stirring beneath the stars.

A few hours later, I caught the first glow of dawn and was ready to meet it. I was back in the yard and working before sunrise.

Anything is possible if you slow down.

HARVEST

August

The festival of Lughnasadh, and dry bracken begins to fall on itself like broken scaffolding. This is the latest in the four-part cycle of dates to mark the passing year, and now we stumble into the harvest and mark the moment with a nod to the old god Lugh. I love these links to the old ways, which were a curiosity at first. It's time to start gathering fat for the winter.

Goats have come down from the hill, and the rough ground is rank with them. I spend part of the morning watching them mingle with the livestock on our neighbour's ground, and finally they come to rest in the whin bushes. Some of them are brindle grey, but most have blaring black-and-white markings which ring in the sunshine. I spy a bearded billy with horns that sweep back from his brow like rutty wheels. He's a fine beast to mark a pagan day. I can almost smell him too at half a mile's distance. Like Lugh, he'll go where he likes. His tribe is gone again by lunchtime and the grass is immeasurably shorter.

Galloway is famous for wild goats, but these are the final remnants of a mighty population which raked across the hills for six centuries. The place was so big in those days that herders would lose their animals in the distant hills; finally so many were lost that a wild population was born. We just ignored them, and they bred a lonely line in the mountains. Goats aren't good in wet weather, and they have nothing to fear in this world but heavy rain in a late spring.

People came to Galloway and were amazed to find the hills were haunted by herds of ownerless livestock. It all seemed crazily inefficient, but we shrugged because the goats had always been there and never done much harm. Perhaps you'd shoot one or two to protect a crop or shy the billies, and I hear the tinkers would steal a kid to raise as tame now and again.

Then the foresters came and the wild herds had a hard time of it. Many goats were destroyed because the moors were being planted and there was no room for passengers in the new plantations. I always think it's a shame to have been so heavy-handed. Many of the cold, draughty forests would be all the more interesting with a goat or two hanging about in them.

Evening. There's darkness by the river and a gurgle of water under the bridge. I look back over my shoulder to the farm. The square, empty buildings stand against the twilight and watch me carefully. A cow is blaring and I know the beast from her bellow.

I am casting into a deep pool where monsters lie. Sea trout lounge in the brown shade during the day and emerge under the cover of darkness. Fishing takes place at night beneath the stars, and the game becomes a secret, black temptation along the riverbank. I feel my line being pulled downstream in a gentle bow; my flies search through the current in slow, steady jerks.

And I have something for the briefest conceivable moment – a livewire connection with a wild fish. It comes to me through the bending rod like a zap; bats hang around me like motes of static. The rod curls dangerously to the bubbling tune of water – and I catch a flare of iridescent silver in the bubbles. Finnock – a wee one! Then the line is slack again and the fish has gone.

The trout came when my mind was elsewhere. I try to cast again. I whip my line overhead in the darkness. I catch my flies on a willow tree behind me and the moment has gone. I am not a natural fisherman, but I cannot ignore old tales of salmon and sea trout in this river. A few remain, but nothing compared to the glut of half a century ago when old Wullie Carson could feed himself easily on wild pink fish throughout the summer and into the autumn. He used to net this river and throw back anything shorter than his arm's length.

I would be breaking the law if I had killed a sea trout for my supper this evening. I would love a thick trout to smoke and lay down for harvest, but all migrant fish must be carefully released to preserve dwindling stocks. Birds call in the gloom; I have truly missed my chance.

*

The oats passed beyond the colour of rich and lovely gold. They were hanging in a grey cloud when Sanny came and said, 'Are you ever gonnae cut that field, son?' I wasn't sure how to time our harvest, but we'd arrived at the 'black' stage. It was time to begin.

I borrowed a sickle and cut bristles of straw until I got a feel for that stuff. It was glossy and thick, and soon there was stubble crackling under my feet. Oats fell and dropped a blizzard of chaff; white flakes like fish scales blew in eddies under the high clouds. Swallows skimmed by and stirred them in a bow wave. Sanny loved swallows and he called them 'the wee boys'. 'The wee boys are lovin' this, son.'

I found bare soil, and light plunged down into the roots to reveal sprigs of nettles and thistles, fat hen and chickweed. Then I stacked the stems in a heap and tied them tightly around the middle with string like a corset. I'd seen it done it books, but I had no idea if this was right. Even Sanny had a machine to do this binding job; he was not sure what to make of my ancient method. He said it looked alright, and I noticed that he was calling my bundle a 'sheaf'. It made a pleasing sight, buxom and wasp-waisted. Soon there were five sheaves, and Sanny explained how to lean them up against each other like a teepee to form a waterproof stook. Barring a monsoon, the crop can stand like this for a fortnight until the wind has blown through the heads and dried the crop for storage.

It took me three hours to make thirty sheaves. It's a tiny harvest, but there was something compulsive about the work. I could hardly take my eyes off the golden stems, and it was exciting to see the soil laid bare after months beneath a rustling canopy. My mind was elsewhere, and I swung the sickle into my index finger. The blade stuck for a moment and the impact stunned my entire skeleton like a tuning fork. There was a bright flash of bone, then deep gouts of blood. The skin hung open like an unzipped pencil case.

'That was bloody careless, son!' shouted Sanny as he sipped at his tea. I pinched the edges of the gash together like stifled lips; blood hung in drips from my fingertips and blots of it fell onto the straw. I felt sick and shaky, but I was working again within the hour. Dirt gathered on the sticky edges of a beige plaster.

Here was another scar to offset nicks and blisters which now run all around my hands. The slit seems to come and go with the weather: sometimes it's a moody blue welt across the back of my hand and people ask what happened, but then the weather changes and it slips away and you'd never know it was there.

I've picked up dark calluses, black nails and cracked fingers in the last few years. I smart with sunburn and ache with strains. A hot bath should relax my tendons, but the water seeps into a network of fresh cuts and scrapes and makes me squeal like a boiling kettle. I'm on my way towards canvas palms and pumice fingers; it's not a painless process. I'm being shaped for purpose, and my brain's changing too.

The scythe is a beautiful tool. It's a snaking bend of wood and steel, held in a bitter pitch of lucid sharpness. Wullie Carson left three scythes hanging from the rafters in his tool shed when he died. I noticed them when we were shown around and I couldn't wait to swing them again. But Wullie's family made a bonfire of his old tools when our offer was accepted and the scythes were burnt along with a host of other paraphernalia. They were just tidying up and couldn't imagine that anyone would ever want wooden tools again.

Those oats were almost a hobby in their early days. I was dipping my toes in the water, being careful not to rely on them until I knew more about the ways of mixed farming. But then the summer was dry, and the grass failed. I took a poor cut of hay and didn't have the chance of cutting again. Neighbours complained that they would run short that winter, and I found myself with nowhere to run. I'd have to produce my own feed or go without. Going without would mean a reduction in stocking, and I couldn't bear to face the loss of a single animal. The oats would have to pull their weight.

I returned with the reaper to speed things up. Chattering teeth skimmed through the oats and they fell in a drift like a rustling wave. Cereals are tougher than grass, and they're not so fussed about rain. If wet weather's coming, you leave the crop standing or you cut it and bind the stems so they're upright. It's not an option to leave them on the ground because the seeds will sprout in no time at all and the crop will be ruined. The weather seemed hard to fathom. I worked cautiously and only cut what I could tie and stack. I cut the crop in narrow sweeps and each one gave me forty sheaves. It took an hour of patient stacking and binding to tidy up in silence, and then I had eight stooks like golden chapels on the stubble.

There used to be machines which did this job in one pass. They were called 'reaper binders'. They passed through the crop and left a trail of perfect sheaves in their wake. Those machines were big and complex, and the important parts were made from canvas and wood. Not many have survived the grind of rot and woodworm, but some live on in the Outer Isles, where crofters are encouraged to keep the old ways alive.

Hand binding calls for a strange twist in the wrist. You bring the string ends round and turn them in a loop, then you pull it tight and the tension sears into your hands in fresh and unrubbed places. New blisters came, and I was raw with the burning slip of string and straw. You can't hurry this job, and the more time you spend, the better the crop will keep. I built beautiful hourglass sheaves and stacked them to spread their skirts so the rain would run down and vanish into the soil. And when I stopped for coffee and a sandwich, the stubbles crackled gently like the sound of a fizzy drink. I sat on spools of golden tape, glossy straw in shining strands.

I rode a peak of my enthusiasm in the early days of that work. I wanted every damn grain in that field. My blood was hot and keen and wild to boast of weights and productivity. What farmer doesn't want to take the most and fastest? There's a hardwired urge to maximise your output, and the landscape reeks of it. That was all very well in the days when we were limited by the power of our own muscles. We used to be happy with stooking and mowing because we couldn't imagine doing any better. We strove to take everything in the knowledge that we could never do it. But my generation has seen the cool efficiency of combine harvesters; I know that it's possible to have it all. I had always had an eye for the birds, and they were part of the driving force behind that crop. But the process of growing made me covetous and greedy; it was all for me.

I'm glad the job was slow because that feeling fell as the work went on through August and into September. Some of the crop had fallen on its side and couldn't be cut. I tried to dig these plants up with a sickle, but there was too much and I made such minor headway. I started to leave small patches here and there where the tractor wheels had flattened the crop. Soon the field looked tatty and amateurish, and I was surprised to find that bothered me.

The heat grew, and I worked on until the air was thick and black darkness piled up over the hills to the west. A few curlews flew in the sunshine, yellow sparks against heavy naval blue. I wondered if they were new birds or whether they were more failures returning from another tragic summer in the north. Then there was a rumble of thunder to match the tractor's roar and rain began to shatter the dry peace of the morning. I told myself that the crop would be safe in the waterproof stooks, but rain like this would destroy a field of hay, and my confidence began to fail. I sprang from the cab and bound the last few sheaves beneath a battering veil of rain which drummed on my back and turned my hair heavy. The water hunted for my blisters and a pink, watery slip dripped from my palms.

It didn't take long for the stooks to turn dull and black beneath the water. They looked awful, and I could hardly ignore the certainty of disaster. The tall, sandy heads were gummed into submission, and the job seemed to be falling apart. A stook fell over and I rushed to repair it, but then the straw was soggy and weak and the bundle flopped like a rag.

And there was rain and still more of it. Hardly a day passed without a smirring veil of cool water. I began to rage at the forecast. I pored over the weather reports which came at first light on the radio. I tried to steal a few hours of dryness here and there to rescue rotting stooks, but the crop smelt of mould. I brought in seventy sheaves and hung them from the rafters in the barn, but there was no breeze in there to dry them and soon they were in a horrible state.

Dry weather came at last. I turned the wet stooks to catch the sun and the harm was undone. I brought the barn sheaves back outdoors and the wind made them crisp and fragrant again. Within a day or two, it was hard to tell which of those sheaves had ever been mouldy. Perhaps the straw was a little tatty, but recovery was miraculous. I'd had little faith in that old system of sheaves and stooks because it all looked too simple: you just tie the crop with string and leave it to stand. I had lost my nerve when the rain came and had tried to think of a better way. I hadn't trusted the stooks, so they corrected me.

Drying the crop is one thing; threshing it is something else. Nowadays the whole job is done by a combine harvesters. The lumbering machines cut the crop, thresh the grain and do all the work in one go. A tractor just drives along beside and carts the grain away by the ton. Before combines there were enormous mills like buses which used to travel around and clean the cereal crops for a whole parish. You dried the crop in sheaves, then you fed them into the mill through a hole in the roof. And if a person fell into that hole, it was curtains. There's no clear idea what came before the big mills, but it's fair to reckon that separating the grains from the strain was a job for old-fashioned elbow grease.

So I would have to clean my oats by hand. I tried a few gadgets and techniques, but nothing was straightforward. The best method was a hand flail which I copied from an old book illustration. Hand flails have been around since the days of Ancient Egypt, and mine took the shape of a five-foot broom handle with a joint towards one end. You throw down a tarpaulin, chuck a sheaf on it and then batter it with the flail until the seeds have fallen off and you can start on another sheaf. The joint helps to amplify the power of every swing, and the end slaps the heads rather than jabs them like a spear. It's as simple and back-breaking as that.

I beat black hell out of those sheaves. Seeds came tumbling out onto the tarpaulin sheet, along with a carnival of beetles and harvestmen, moths and ladybirds. Soon it was pooling in the dips, and I could run my hands through it and start to weigh my progress.

Threshing was a slow and steady slog. I took the best from every sheaf, but it was hard to resist wasting mugfuls of the seed. I needed dry weather for this work because rain clogged the seeds and made the job sticky. I picked my moments and threshed when it was dry, and a good breeze blew the chaff away in a blizzard of beige teardrops until the field was papery and crinkled and the seeds lay clean and crisp like beans.

I watched the horizon all the while, scanning for the return of rain. Hills come and go from view, and the old landscape becomes a forecast. If I can see Bengairn, things are fine. I have about half an hour before I need to stop when

Maidenpap starts to blur and turn grey. If I lose sight of Buittle and Kirkennan, moisture is imminent.

If you were to measure my progress against the value of my gains, the comparison would be depressing. I can manage about sixty pounds of bagged, clean seed in an hour. The figure rises to a hundred when I have help. I could work at my desk and earn enough to buy twice as much, but I've always been happier to spend time in lieu of money.

My main consolation is that now I've got stiff calluses and my hands no longer bleed.

The sky was thick with swallows. I counted 170 on the telegraph wires below the house. The yellowhammers have produced a hearty brood of youngsters, and there are greenfinches and goldfinches swarming like ants over the fallen crop.

*

We bought two pigs when we came to this place. They found fun in a broad paddock behind the byre. The weaners ran in curly loops beneath the irises with their eyes rolled back and their ears akimbo. They camped outdoors like children in the half-light of midsummer, and their snores rolled across the yard. Swallows had rushed over their heads in a reeling kaleidoscope of sound and colour, and the pigs had been part of it all. Their bodies laid down fat for the winter but their minds thought of nothing but fun. Of course we loved them.

The march of autumn and the constant grind of their snouts had pulled this paradise to mud. The ground became mush, and the growing pigs were surly and short-tempered. Exploratory nuzzles suddenly felt sharp and painful; the beasts were settling in for winter as mature, well-grown animals. They lost their sense of humour and became vessels for protein and fat. The impish darlings of high summer were gone, and it was suddenly hard to face the reality of what would come next. Producing animals can be so consuming that it's easy to lose track of the terminus.

Their carcasses were strange and unfamiliar. The life rushed out of them and took everything we knew and loved. Stripped of their klutzy, fumbling charm, our pigs were just pork. Toasting their memory, we drank deep slugs of whisky and lifted the cold shapes onto tables in the yard. We'd bought tobacco and rolled cigarettes with trembling fingers, keen for some dizzy escape. Slightly elevated above the granite setts by alcohol and nicotine, we chatted with noisy lightness and began the chore.

Steel blades stripped them down into pieces. A weak autumnal sun lit up our work as webs of geese passed high overhead, moving south and Solway-bound. Vats of steaming water were brought to soften the same bristles we'd scratched and patted all summer. A brutally sharp knife scraped away the hair and revealed leathery crackling beneath. They'd been saddleback pigs – black with a band of pink around their shoulders. As we rubbed the skins, black pigment came away with the hair like damp crêpe paper. Their bodies were pink and mannish.

Joints were dismantled and contours were pared into tidy bunches of muscle. The bones themselves were startlingly white, porcelain shapes in a mass of meat. My hands were sticky with the season's fat.

We worked on the carcasses for a day and divided them into less recognisable parts. These were hung on hooks, and soon it was hard to tell what had been where. We began to process these parts as the temperature dropped and the cooler nights chilled the fat into firm, workable layers. The bacon cured in vats of sugar and salt. Hams hung from the rafters while we brewed up brines and cures which were mixed with juniper and peppercorns. Bags of apples came in from the trees and hung by the kitchen until the house smelled sweet and clean. Soon there were links of sausages and bowls of waxy brawn cooling in the shed.

I mourned the pigs, but they were long gone and there was little time for sadness – it's no mean feat to capture and preserve three hundredweight of meat. And we could've done more – we could've split the toes and scraped the tails, a thousand little chores to eke out every last blob of fat and gelatin. These are the old-fashioned ways. We focused on what was doable: chops, hams, hocks and bacon. There's no 'Friday at five p.m.' deadline in this job; pigs should be killed when the cold weather comes and the meat should be stowed for the dark days of winter. There is a binding relevance to that simple fact.

I rejoiced to bring in the hay – we sat in the half-light and drank cider beneath a mountain of our sun-dried grass. The rain was surely coming, but we'd stolen a dry day so the cattle could be fed. If that moment had been joy, the death of those pigs was an equivalent and unavoidable sorrow. It's easy to ignore the weather and the seasons: modern man is always warm, fed and comfortable. I'm grateful to the pigs for that pull on the thread; the reminder that life is always moving in a turning wheel of boom and bust, joy and tragedy.

When the pigs were dead and stowed, I had time to think about the cattle. Pigs are made on a short turnover – a headlong sprint to the freezer which leaves no survivors. New distilleries often produce gin to generate some income while they wait for the whisky to mature. The pigs were our gin, and it'd be years before the cattle were ready to go.

It was consoling to know that the pigs had never seen the coming of their death. They say that pigs are clever and know more than they let on, but they didn't see it coming. Pigs should fast the night before they're killed so their bellies are empty. I don't understand the science, but it's supposed to help the meat set. I nursed a growing sense of unease during that long, dark night. I dwelled on ideas of betrayal and cursed myself for the brutality of it all. But the pigs were simply wondering why they hadn't been fed. Death came in an instant, and only that moment was spoiled for them. I had shied away from the idea of my Galloways hanging by their heels in an abattoir. But that could be any of us. Nobody knows what's coming next.

*

After two weeks I'd cleared a big sweep of the oats. I pushed on and began to pile sacks of clean grain in the shed. The reaper clattered away in the standing crop. Sanny brought a pal to see it working. The dogs ran out to see Sanny, but they weren't sure about this new man. They hung around Sanny and he clapped them as we spoke. Sanny's pal was in his forties and he'd never seen a reaper. He was mildly curious, but he had somewhere to rush away to afterwards and his visit felt like a favour to the old boy.

Farm machinery is notoriously short-lived. Some machines make a difference and become celebrities; many are just forgotten. My reaper was made by the famous Massey Ferguson company, but it was an obsolete model and spare parts were unheard of. That's why I got it cheap. The basic mechanism would ring a bell with anyone who farmed up to (but not after) the 1970s.

After five years I'd built up quite a collection of old and rusting metal. The assortment had no connection to any one era, and it was bound together by nothing more than convenience and geography. Collectors like to specialise in a particular manufacturer and go crazy to hunt down every detail of authenticity. I had picked my kit on price, and I refused to travel further than Lancaster or Stirling. Anything beyond those outer reaches was too far. My machinery spanned over forty years of progress and development, boasting dependable British names like Bamford, Ransomes and Ferguson. I took Sanny and his pal out into the field and they solemnly watched me drop the clutch and let the blades away. Sanny always enjoyed that moment when the knives began to fly. His pal stole a quick glance at his watch.

My grandfather might have been particularly cussed and stubborn, but he fought the arrival of combine harvesters for many years. He was adamant that the new machines worked too fast. In his mind, they didn't dry the straw as well as stooking did, so he worked out a middle ground between old and new. He would cut his oats like I did, binding the stems into stooks and leaving them to dry in the wind until they were crisp and clean. When the weather was right, he'd then dismantle the heaps, cut open the bundles and spread them out on the grass for the combine harvester to pick them up. He swore that the straw was better and the job was altogether superior.

But combine harvesters are designed to make a farmer's life easier. My grandfather's approach seemed to fight progress by making it doubly labour intensive. He was being a stick-in-the-mud, and he was finally overruled. The combine harvester was allowed to do the whole job, but it must have stuck in his throat.

I reached the end of the row and looked back over my shoulder. Sanny was showing his pal one of my sheaves. I turned off the tractor and walked over as they handled the crop and found the oats were beautifully dry. The straw crackled like newspaper in their hands, and Sanny's pal was pretty impressed. We had his full attention, but then he asked how long the work had taken me, and I said two weeks at full stretch. He laughed out loud because the only measure of a good job is how fast you've done it. My extra care and time might have produced something of higher quality, but that margin was irrelevant because it was slow. He hasn't been back to visit, and I'm not going to lose sleep over that.

The rain came again, and I took a sheaf of oats to the cattle because it occured to me that I was breaking my back over this crop without any hint of how it would go down with the end consumers. It would be several weeks before they'd need additional feeding, but I couldn't resist a test run, my summer's work laid before them like a ceremonial offering.

There had been rain all day, but the sky was breaking up into a sodden sunset. Juicy clouds flew over the wet yard and the stones sang in a trickle of water. I looked out over the moss and found veils of blue sweat swelling up from the forest. The hills were black, but the cattle were bathed in a pink, hearty sun. I hefted the sheaf under my arm and set out for them.

Wildflowers glimmered neatly around my beasts; fuzzy globes of scabious and gorgeous waxy stars of Parnassus grass. Both were being boosted by cattle grazing, and bumblebees cruised heavily through them. The beasts didn't show much interest at first, but finally I hooked one with the offering. She nuzzled the straw, then reached out a long blue tongue and pulled the bundle from my hand. Soon there were two cows munching the yellow straws with every sign of satisfaction. The seeds hung in a nodding web, and soon there were burps and gurgles below the grinding crump of molars. Then a third cow came to see what was happening; there was a demand for more. I read it and laughed because it seemed so clear as to be almost spoken.

I can focus on the smallest thing at times like that. I find sparks of wild and buckling clarity, and I start at the joy of ever-decreasing details. I can hang for half an hour on the quiet shuffling hiss of cattle eating hay. And if I can find the finest edge of that awareness, I become a lightweight. I'm drunk on the sight of byre dust swirling in a shaft of sunlight or the rasp of a brush on a granite floor. That kind of pleasure can make the hours sing, and I reach to be better at it because then I belong in the precision of that moment. I never reckoned to find this strength, but it's a product of deep slowness and patience. I used to marvel at the folk who lived their quiet, lonely lives in the hills. If this is how they saw the world, it must've been easy.

The cattle consume me, and then I'm free again and I look forward to the next phase of the crop rotation. I can't wait to serve up turnips and swedes, and to see the ground humming with more life and excitement on a bigger scale.

Even in those moments of optimism, it's hard to see curlews in that future. My shoulders slump, and the sunset dims. This place will be permanently altered by the loss of curlews. It feels like a red line which can't be crossed.

But then I think of old books and find other red lines which we crossed years ago. People mourned the coming of electricity to the hill farms, the loss of heavy horses and the rush towards diesel tractors. The cattle push and nudge me as I stand above a far horizon of commercial forest, wind turbines and clean, emerald grassland. My ancestors dreamed of progress, but they'd grind their teeth to see this place as it is now. They'd call it wrecked and foul, and I feel that rage on their behalf, but even in this final extremity I still find plenty to love here.

I've spoken to people who say we should pull out of the hills and let them heal. They want the wild, and they ask me how I can love Galloway when it's been broken and twisted into sickness. I try and imagine these hills as they were in their original state: birchwoods and the bark of pine trees running to the furthest horizon. The glimpse of a fox can jangle my brain, so it's hard to resist the tempting howl of wolves over the yard at dusk, but nostalgia can't pay the bills any more than hills of cattle can. My heart breaks for Galloway, but I'll never leave this place, where the only tradition that truly endures is change.

I've been raked by the loss of old things ever since I first looked around me. As an adult, I was stifled by fears for the future and my own family. Then farming pressed me to move and think in slow motion, teasing me with reminders of my tiny unimportance. I had slowed down my life to keep pace with old cattle which don't look back or forward and breathe only the latest turn of the wind.

Suddenly I know that the best of this place is not past or future, but now.

MART

October

Samhain, and the end of the year's life. The world has slumped into cobwebs and fallen grass. The myrtle sinks to the redness of wine and grouse stand up like bottles in the peat.

The easterly wind is cold and it fills the yard with dry grass. The fences are festooned with strandy bunting which trembles like a madman's hair. Old folk call this grass 'flying bent' because it flies away in the first good winds of autumn, and I follow miles of it trailing from the telephone wire which bows above the hill.

This grass was red and thick a week ago, but the rain and the sinking temperatures have stripped away those autumnal colours. The hills are shedding their jammy tang, and now they are cold and grey beneath a flat winter light. The sky darkens with the rush of flying grass and new faces have come to surf above the open ground.

Owls are hunting over the moor, sweeping up the dust of summer. I look up from some chore and find a bird staring into my eyes like a hypnotist; blaring yellow discs invite me to swoon or obey. This hunter is busy and he lands for a moment on the dyke between the moor and the stubbles. He looked big on the wing but his fluff and volume is just for show; you could fit him in a coffee cup. Blown in like some piece of wasted grass, this bird has followed those easterly winds from Norway or Sweden to be here at this, our moment of final collapse. We are tired, but all this is news to him.

We go to see curlews by the shore and sit in the pub where fishing boats are leaning on the clicking mud. We watch small birds hustling for trade amongst the mussels. They rise in shoals and twinkle against the famous grey hills of the Lake District; dunlin and knot move like winter swallows against the vast sky.

The Solway is broad and strange in its emptiness. Stare over miles of quicksand and sliding mud, and light spans the pooling water like a mackerel's back. It's deadly and cool, and the tide pours in from the far horizon at a gallop. Stand still and you'll sink in the quaking sand. The kindly mud will slip around your knees and give comfort as the tide climbs your belly and pools in the nock of your gullet. The last thing you'll ever see is a lid of grey salt water.

Who can say what lies in that sand? I knew a fisherman who ran nets in the sea and drove out on a tractor at the passing of each tide. His son rode with him, and the boy would keep the tractor moving so the wheels wouldn't stick. The man would check his nets, and the boy would drive round and round in tight circles until they were ready for home. One day they drove out and saw a dark shape lying in the sand. Curiosity won them over, and they pulled out for a closer look. A mile beyond their nets, they found a boat lying on its side. The fisherman reckoned it was fifty feet long, with a cab and a steamer engine. God knows where it had come from, but they marked the exact location and planned to come back the next day with saws and a trailer to salvage what they could. But it was gone by the next low tide and never came up again. So it's hard to guess how many boats are rumbling around in that soup, revealed and then hidden again with every gliding tide. It's a fitting place for half-seen birds which fly beside flounders and shoals of dozy mullet.

Our eyes are drawn to the crows picking up mussels from the beach and dropping them on parked cars like vandals. They hope to crack the shells, but they'd do better on a rock.

A few curlews stand beneath the falling mussels; they do not panic or fluster. They're rooted in the mud and their toes have become anchors. They see me through the steamy pub windows, but we are not familiar. Perhaps these curlews were hatched in Finland or Russia. The last of our own have gone down to Ireland or Brittany to lick their wounds by the same sea.

*

My father stepped through the door into the mart. I rode on his shoulders and breathed in sharp smells of cow shit, sawdust and cigarette smoke. I was five years old and I'd never seen so many people in my life. There must have been forty men gathered in the gloom beneath that conical roof.

He pushed into the middle of the crowd. Gates clanged, doors slammed and my mouth hung open on its hinge. There was a smell of onion gravy, stovies and stale beer from the pub over the street.

Then my feet were resting on the metal frame which ran around the edge of the auction ring. A big white bull turned in circles around a sawdust arena, rolling his puffy pink eyes and huffing like a train. The auctioneer sent up an endless drone which made my head hum, numbers in patterns and offers and queries, then tangles and backwards and laughter and on. Two clerks kept pace with him, and a runner came in from the office with bloodshot eyes and a fag stuck to his lip.

The bull turned his ears and hated it; he suffered a man to tap his back and keep him turning for everyone to see. After months of hidden silence on the blue hills, this would've been a sensory overload for the stacked batches of cattle which bellowed and shat in the sheds behind the podium. Strip lights cast a black shadow on the sawdust below the bull's belly. I wondered what we looked like to him.

The hammer fell at last; not a price but a list of numbers. Five-nine-three-oh. The bull lurched out of his ring, another gate opened and another bull came through. I looked down on the men around me through a mist of tobacco smoke. Their faces were found beneath a moving carpet of flat caps. A friend of my father's came and stood by us, and he winked up at me. Crushing embarrassment: a reminder that I was just a child.

It's easy to see meat when your beast is dead and skinless, but I challenge you to pick out 'good' from 'less good' when it's standing upright in a thick, baggy skin. Some of the butchers in Castle Douglas can measure up a walking beast without breaking step. They'll give you a scarily accurate stab at value and cost off the back of a fag packet as the auctioneer drones on and pigeons clatter in the rafters.

A few breeds attract more money because they're famous and customers are willing to pay a little more for the kudos. There's always a market for Galloway beef, but nobody mentions riggits on their marketing bumf. The name is too obscure to add value, but it's not too much to hope that'll change. It's lucky that the farmers who worked so hard to rescue riggit Galloways from extinction had their heads screwed on. They know that markings don't matter when the skin's off and the frame is hanging from a hook. Riggits are traditional, stocky animals, but they have good flesh in all the right places. That's where live animals start to be recognised as joints and are measured on meat yield. Butchers count the number of steaks they can slice out of a long back; they peer at the legs and hunt for the rump that is square and plump.

I didn't know any of this when I began to look at Galloways. I saw nothing but uniformity, and the fine details went far over my head. Back when I was dithering about cattle, I went to a stock-judging competition laid on for young farmers by the Galloway Cattle Society. I was baffled by a relentless procession of identical black animals. I tried to choose 'the best', but the beasts blurred together and each new heifer overlaid the last in my memory. They were all just black cows, and I wondered how it could ever be possible to compare one beast against another. That was one of the reasons why I took to riggit Galloways in the early days; it's easy to tell them apart. I felt like an excitable teenage boy for having based my love on looks above substance.

Once they'd come to me, I checked and fed them every day. My beasts became so familiar that I began to memorise their shapes. It didn't take me long to home in on conformation, and soon I was conjuring up fine details of length and girth. I thought one of my calves was the most stunning beast I'd ever seen, but she grew into a cow with many failings; she was skinny at the back and narrow along the spine. Meanwhile, one of the ugliest heifers filled into beefy perfection. Her markings were all wrong, but she made a stunning silhouette. I was learning to balance beauty with function. If I wanted to produce good cattle, I'd have to bring both together in a single beast.

I first saw that perfect blend on a cold, rain-soaked day in Lancashire. I'd gone down to look at a bull, and the farmer had mentioned in passing that he was going to take three young heifers to the sale at Castle Douglas in October. I asked to see them on a whim. I had no reason to buy another animal. Besides, I was broke again. It was just window shopping.

We splashed across wet fields and found the beasts in a gang beneath a bank of gorse with their heads buried in thick cover. One of them turned to look, and it was love at first sight. She was exactly what I wanted; the other two were just cows. I felt a swell of pride to realise my progress – cattle were not all the same, and some were clearly better than others.

She was smaller than the other two, but she had a kind of well-mannered arrogance which spoke aloud that she was boss. Thick, tough and square as a Mini Cooper, she tossed her head in the smirr and shook off a mist of water. I saw all the room she had for growth and smiled at the thickness which seemed to be unfolding in her legs and over her back. Deep veils of hair and skin wobbled across her breast like a greedy basset hound. Some Galloways have long, trailing faces which make them look sad and ponderous. Some people like it, but others see it as a fault. I think Galloways are meant to have short, punchy heads, and this heifer was a case in point. Her nose rolled around into her chin with a smooth, gentle sweep like a boxing glove.

I didn't give the other two riggits a second glance, and I walked around my favourite in a state of high excitement. It was doubly satisfying to see that her markings were ideal. I've always hankered after a dark riggit heifer, and this animal was a shiny blue-black – I heard the farmer explain that her father was a bull called Black Grouse, a stunning beast from the West Country who I knew well by reputation.

Her head was almost solid black, but she had white 'tears' below her eyes and a white chinstrap which ran below her ears and under her chin. There are no hard and fast rules, but this to me was what a riggit should look like. My first heifers had been a punt – I loved them, but I'd been working in the dark.

If I could buy this girl, it would be a concrete step towards a definite goal. Here was a chance to steer my project based on my own experience and learning. For the first time, I felt that I knew what I was doing.

You don't just come out and say, 'I want that cow.' That's far too simple. I worked around the subject and looked for a time at one of the other heifers. Then I circled back in due course and I began a conversation which allowed us to pass near the idea of a private sale. This kind of talk is a thing of beauty when it's done right. You could read a transcript and have no idea what is being said as two people feel and probe for a deal. A thousand conversations take place under the veil of idle chat. Despite a good start, I blundered and pushed my point into the open. The farmer blinked at the sudden clarity; he'd been wanting see how I'd approach it. But it was all for the birds anyway because these heifers were all going to the sale, and that was that.

The Annual Show and Sale of Belted and White Galloway Cattle is a landmark in the Galloway year. People come from all over the world to see our cattle sold, and the brick yards hum with excitement on the Market Hill in Castle Douglas. Most of this buzz wells up around belted Galloways, the most famous black-and-white beasts in Scotland. The finest belted Galloway bull might sell for less than a tenth of what you'd pay for a high-octane commercial breed at Perth, but there's nothing part-time or hobbyish at Castle Douglas. Big exports go across the world, and the bulls are polished to a glassy sheen of perfection.

Speak to some of the breeders at Castle Douglas and they'll list the many virtues of Galloway cattle. Some are working towards top-notch beef; others need hardy livestock for conservation projects like mine. There are all kinds of reasons to take the day seriously, but it's surprising how many folk lean on a vague feeling that native breeds are fundamentally important. You find the same words and ideas when people gather to play folk music or take part in old dances. Maybe it's helpful to abandon yourself and be part of an old tradition sometimes, even if you can't put your finger on why that continuity and repetition is so valuable. And there's a nice anonymity to the big breeders and the famous herds. They might rise for a decade and enjoy success with their animals, but celebrity doesn't last in this business. My grandfather was a big player at this sale in the 1970s, but his name isn't mentioned today. Even the most famous names can soon be lost, and it's humbling to see those cattle as the sum of a thousand nameless contributions.

White Galloways are often tacked on to the end of the belted Galloway sale, and a few beasts are sold once the main roar of excitement has passed. It seems unfair to relegate the white beasts to play second fiddle behind their belted cousins, but these are the quirks of fancy and taste.

In a bid to raise their profile, the farmer had lobbied to sell his trio of riggit heifers in the midst of this excitement. After years in the wilderness, these beasts would be the first pedigree riggits ever sold at Castle Douglas. The Riggit Galloway Cattle Society hoped that this would generate some much-needed publicity and interest. The farmer was granted his wish, but the heifers were tacked on after the white Galloways like an afterthought. It was a telling reminder that riggits occupy a small corner of a very marginal world, and their presence is often merely tolerated.

*

The pigs were gone, and bits of them hung in the sheds. We celebrated the first good snow with slices of their bacon, and it was unlike any meat I'd ever tasted. The fat melted into a sugary, toothsome pool around our bread, and it thrilled me. I looked back on memories of generic commercial bacon and suddenly realised that it was just wet, salty paper by comparison. Pigs have suffered the same fate as cattle as producers rush towards speed and volume, and flavour is sidelined. Our bacon came from age-old, outdoor-reared pigs.

I began to strain towards the day when I will carve a slice of home-bred beef. It'll be worth waiting for. If quality speaks for itself then I've got fingers crossed we'll have no trouble selling it.

The yard was quiet without the pigs. They left a hole in this place. I looked down on their empty paddock and their old diggings. Part of their pen had been Wullie Carson's old dump, but the trash had grown over and we didn't know it was there until the pigs ripped up the turf like a damp scab. Wullie Carson had been tipping his junk over that dyke for years, out of sight and out of mind. When the dump got too big, he'd set fire to it and then dump more on top.

The best I could do was pick up the obvious top layer. I found mats of melted trash. I broke them up and hauled them away to the council dump. I realised that this had been a dump for generations, and the layers of rubbish had grown like rings on a growing tree. The pigs organised a full inventory of lost litter, and they quarried the trash for days.

At first they showed me glass bottles. Broken shards peered through the mud like dragon's teeth, and I hurried to clean them up in case their snouts were slashed by the glittering edges. Below the shattered trash lay troves of pristine glass: a dozen immaculate beer bottles from the long-defunct brewery in Dumfries, heavy brown jugs of DOMESTOS lying strewn beside lemonade from McMichaels of Eastriggs (also defunct).

They were beautiful and so perfectly preserved that they might have been emptied yesterday.

And then the pigs brought me empty jars of lime marmalade, meat paste and Brylcreem. So I was on the trail of Teddy boys, but soon we were deeper into cork-stoppered jugs of liniments and unctions. I stumbled upon the muddy shell of a toy Austin 7, then found spokes which might have come from the real thing. And there were boot soles and mess tins, horseshoes and tough fibres of leather tack. I found a gas lamp and several earthenware jars which had been made in Castle Douglas. Soon the pigs and I were passing beyond the Great War, back into discs of blue-and-white china which dressed the gears of a bicycle and the breech of a shotgun. I kicked away the clods and revealed the head of a hoe and the hands of a clock. This would have dazzled me in the old days. I'd have rushed to preserve it all, and I'd have made a system to log and record every detail because it pointed back to oldness and that was my weakness.

But now I'm a little more stand-offish. Wullie Carson threw that stuff away (although not very far), and the only value I can find in old bottles or broken enamel taps is that they're here in this place which is fast becoming mine. I picked out a few things that pleased me: a jar of Jardine's Tooth Powder and an empty bottle of stout. They give me a sense of people passing through. I carted the rest to the dump. I'm less inclined to carry passengers these days.

*

I went to see the perfect heifer in her pen on the morning of the sale. The auction house flooded my head with memories. I rediscovered that blend of straw and onion gravy, but the tang of cow piss was even nippier without cigarette smoke to mellow it. I was always amazed to see hard men cowed by that smoking ban. The night before the law was passed, they'd grumbled and sworn, saying, 'The bastards'll never stop me.' But many a jeering heavy was found lurking meekly in the beer garden with his fag the next afternoon.

I found her in the dead time while the belted Galloways were being shown and compared. She stood quietly with her sisters and I chatted to the farmer as I wrung my sale catalogue into a mush of nervousness. He knew I was bound to bid, so I didn't even try to hide my anxiety. They would come on last, shortly before the store cattle and the commercial beasts.

Then I took a seat on the steps and watched cattle come and go. I saw grand heavy bulls and wild cows which stamped and bellowed at the stockman as their calves wailed and turned their ears back. The auctioneer's voice droned through the loudspeakers, shoals of numbers like the starlings which cast their shadows through the mottled skylights overhead. People sidled carefully through the ranks. There was a current of heads and gossip-filled eddies, littered with coffee and scotch pies in greasy paper. If you're used to silence and the same routine, the big sale casts a long shadow.

The lots passed slowly. A belted Galloway bull went for 6,000 guineas, an old way of paying which gives a few pennies in every pound to the auctioneer, and his halter bristled with rosettes. The crowd thinned once he'd been through, and the people slacked away as we approached the end of the sale. I sprang to a gap on the ringside when it opened for a moment, then gripped the wooden rail as it closed again. I'd staked my claim and held it like a tick.

Any fool can buy a cow, but the experience is meaningless without fine attention to protocol. After several centuries of determined Presbyterianism in Galloway, this is a masterclass in suppressed emotion. It's forbidden to show any expression as the bids are made. You shrug and suck your teeth. If you can attract the auctioneer's attention by throbbing a vein on your forehead, then you're starting to get the idea. Tradition dictates that all faces around the ring should be left utterly blank; allowances are sometimes made for expressions of despair and boredom. In this game, triumph and defeat run in screaming riot behind a screen of pessimistic indifference.

I worked hard to wipe every crease of expression from my face. Deep breaths. I stared at the sawdust as the first riggit came in and jogged in a wobbling trot around the ring. The auctioneer reminded us that these were the first pedigree riggit Galloways ever to be sold through the ring in Castle Douglas. I fought the rush and wondered how many riggits have passed through this ring over the last century without any official recognition or endorsement. They would have been bizarre throwback store cattle, sold with a shrug of confusion. But yesterday's freak had become today's pedigree.

The first heifer sold, and not for big money. She was my least favourite of the three, but I'd just seen belted Galloway heifers sell for almost three times as much simply because their stripe was around the middle rather than along the back. So much for logic.

Then my darling entered the ring. I tried to count backwards. Nobody wants to jump in too soon, and the auctioneer began to lower the starting price. I stared at the ground and pretended not to care as my pulse roared in my ears. A child laughed and the crowd continued to dribble away through the open doors.

Then bidding began. Somebody started us off, but I couldn't look. I only knew that they were behind me and to the right. I ignored it and caught the auctioneer's eye with sheer willpower; he must have felt the fury coming off me. His hair would've been sizzling with it. I'd set a budget, but that was exceeded in a short tit-for-tat exchange of 100 guineas a time. I battled every impulse to scream, to jump up on the edge of the ring and shout, 'That's my heifer and you can all FUCK OFF!' I strove to focus that nerve-snapping roar into a single, gentle nod of my head as if nothing could matter less and I was already thinking about what I would have for lunch.

The hammer fell at 900 guineas. The auctioneer announced my name to a clerk without having asked it. I'd never seen either of those men before, but they knew me because they knew my father. A tall, smiling guy from Connemara was standing beside me and he turned to shake my hand and said, 'That's a grand wee beast.' He hadn't even realised I was bidding until the gavel fell. I'd won.

*

Geese came down to the stubbles. At first they were greylags from the hill lochs, but soon there were foreign birds riding the cool winds again. There were white-fronted and pink-footed geese from the far north, and they cried at the prickle of stars. Leaves blew in the birches, and the birds rode against dark hills as I rose from my bed and stirred the embers of the stove back to life.

I'm used to the gentle flash and turn of summer light. Shortening days bring darkness and blunt, heavy birds which wail and natter in the gloom. Subtlety dies in these riotous months when large gaggles waddle like sheep across the glen, and the ganders hiss and watch me beadily. When the time comes for them to travel, they shake themselves into powerful vees which run for miles across the sky. The birds take it in turns at the apex of the vee because that's the hardest flying, suited only to the strongest and most dominant. Air wears them down like a plough point and they're exhausted by the drag, so often they'll drop back and others will take their place. Once the air is broken, the team flies in the slipstream and they all find the work less trying. It's hard to forge a new path and much easier to fly where others have flown before. I know that feeling well.

Now they land and stand and turn their suspicion on a fox trotting along the burn banks. I think it's the same character who dined on curlew flesh in the summer, but now he has smooled up a thick coat again and I can't be sure. He's half a mile away and there's time to find the rifle, but for now I sit and watch him and think back to foxes I've known in the flesh.

It bothers me that he should be my enemy, not least because killing him would do nothing to help the curlew. I'd have to kill him at the right moment and stand ready to kill the others which come behind him, and that's beyond my power. Old Wullie would've killed him on sight and claimed he had it coming, but I'm working out what to carry forward and what to abandon from the old ways. I don't crave the fox's death like an older man might, but I see how it could help. And I know that if we're serious about keeping curlews in this place, we'll need to toughen up and grow some of that ancient killing callus.

Small birds fell on the oat stubbles like ash from a hill fire. The pleasure of this work is the year-round flare of bird life. They doubled and then doubled again in their numbers. I saw all sorts come to the harvested field, and then they were joined by dark and sodden doos which cruised through the rain like plashy rags. Then I looked onto the field to find a queue of seventy yorlins gurning in the smirr along the dyketops.

There were greenfinches and linnets in that listed mess, and they flared away like sparks from a grinder as a merlin came off the moss and tried his hand with the wind behind him.

He failed, but he came back two days later as I worked to fettle our cattle crush. The old machine was cheap, and I saw a chance to strip away the denty old panels and replace them with wooden slats. Water fell steadily, and I turned to find birds writhing in the grass behind me. The merlin had caught his linnet, and the little singer screamed as his back was opened up to the rain.

I watched the merlin's blue wings fluttering. His yellow toes kneaded at the meat and the black nails were buried in down. I know that the merlin is a cousin of the kestrel; he is *Falco columbarius*. The linnet is a finch like a yorlin or a twite. I try to switch off that information. The Victorians adored linnets and sold them as songbirds in ornamental cages. They also hated merlins and killed every one they could find. Maybe I should enslave the prey and drop a shovel on the predator. I ignore that knowledge too.

Rain drums on my hood as I sit back and drink in fine details of light and feather. I have recalibrated my brain to draw goodness from things which would have scarcely stirred a raised eyebrow in the past. I am becoming an efficient consumer, and this is a feast to fatten me for days.

*

The sheds are groaning with grain, and we have rats. I saw one last week, and now I see them often. They run under the doors and leave greasy tracks on the granite steps. Cast torch-light through the dark sheds and the timbers glitter with shining eyes. Our work's been so messy that we've drawn them in from miles around, and now they squat in our middens and build nests in the oat straw. The farm is their oyster, and they're joined by litters of mice and starlings, jackdaws, pigeons and sparrows. I shift the oats into steel containers where they'll be safe, but this place is full of feeding. I told Sanny about the rats and he shuddered. He hates rats; the vermin scamper through his nightmares.

I must have heard this story a dozen times, and this was one of the few whose details didn't change with every retelling. As a boy, Sanny had found an empty water barrel full of rats. They'd fallen in and were running around the bottom like race cars round a track. Of course the rats should die, but Sanny was undecided on how best to kill them. He dithered about drowning them. He wondered if he could borrow a dog. In the end, he reckoned that his best bet would be to stick them with a pitchfork. Sanny rushed off to find a fork, and the rats ran round and round in a sweaty circle while they waited.

It was hard to pick a target. The rats kept running and they made Sanny dizzy. His first jab was delivered with such force and enthusiasm that it missed the rats and the fork stuck in the bottom of the barrel. Before he could think to pull it out, every single rat in that barrel had climbed up the fork tines, up the shaft, and was running over Sanny's neck to freedom. Sixty years have passed, but Sanny still can't say 'rat' unless it's a 'fucking rat'.

I hate rats too, but I try to be pragmatic. I accepted old weeds in the summer, knowing that they brought insects and a boom of life. It'd be mad of me to smile at nettles and docks, then strive for the annihilation of 'vermin'. Friends advised me to lay poison for the rats and mice, but I couldn't bring myself to do it. Poison grows arms and legs of its own, and it finds its way into unexpected corners. I was happy to shoot them or trap them, and we had a busy afternoon digging them out with a terrier. Sanny loved that, but he was always up on a wooden crate when the brutes broke cover.

If the animals should be dead, then so be it. I'd kill them, and that would be the end of it. I wanted to live alongside this place, and I'd first chosen curlews as a point of focus. I was nearly blinded by those birds, and I could've ignored everything else. I asked my cattle to stir a bow wave across the farm, so maybe I should accept a few rats, knowing that they're part of a bigger system. I didn't want them in my kitchen, right enough, and I couldn't afford to have them eat the whole crop, but I could find a balance.

Now we have owls hunting the yard after dark, and a weasel has set up his shop in a heap of old grain sacks. He makes a fair go of those rats and, my God, do they shriek when they hear him coming. And a falcon visits to hunt the starlings, and a hawk destroys the pigeons.

We bought an empty shell: hollow granite walls and tin roofs. There's life in the old place yet.

ENDINGS

November

I have sold an animal, and now I see the first wink of income after five years.

We struck a deal on Thursday, and arrangements were made to collect the beast at first light the following morning.

A thick frost fell overnight; I pick my way into the yard beneath a gallery of stars to find the quad bike. The shed door rolls back on its runners and wild duck pour past overhead. They've come from inland, and now they rush down to the Solway to roost. They're whooping with the joy of it, and I think Fergus rides with them.

The lorry is coming in less than an hour. The cattle pens are open, but we are three fields away on unfamiliar ground. I clasp a half bale of hay between my knees and trundle out from the shed into the icy fields, feeling my way in the darkness. A cold yellow glow provides backlighting to the Lake District – the shapes of Skiddaw and Buttermere glower over the Solway as I gain altitude and pause to open each gate in turn, leaving dark fingerprints on the icy bars. I reach the fields where the beasts have been left and begin to shout. The cattle are suckers for my call, and the scent of hay will draw them from a long distance.

The quad bike rolls to a halt. Suddenly I am surrounded by animals – great broadsides of black, steaming hair beneath the stars. The cattle move half-seen around me, silhouetted against the sea, black shapes breathing sweet cud into the stillness. Folds of land have conspired to hide every spark of electric light. The quad bike aside, this scene might have been playing out in the eighteenth century.

The beasts are keen; I push the bike ahead and shout and wave the dry grass. They take the bait and crowd behind me, but some freak of excitement and enthusiasm spurs their curiosity into an avalanche. They toss their heads and begin to stampede down the hill. I pick up speed and they come along with me, puffing and rollicking beside the bike. They feed on their own excitement; they kick their heels and roll their eyes until the frozen soil fairly rumbles beneath them. Clods of icy mud fly against the stars and I am driving inside a heaving mass of living meat – twelve tons of beef bellowing and rumbling within arm's reach.

On the final stretch to the pens, the broad landscape opens out before me in the gloaming – a rolling spread of whin, oak wood and white moorland for thirty miles. I shout and cheer the beasts on, and there are hot tears streaking back into my ears. These are my animals and this is our place. They are made of my grass and the feed I have worked to give them; hours of labour and weeks of sweating pain have made them fat and valuable. I am deliciously glad that we have done this ourselves because every inch of this flaring joy is our own, and I wish my wife was here to see it. The beasts run ahead of me, and soon I am tossing the hay in the pens. The trap is closed behind them. They mill happily around me in the muck as I shut the gate and prepare for the cattle lorry.

I don't rush off to work at my desk as the sun finally comes up and burns the frost off the rushes; I am already working. I look to the cattle and think of how long it took me to win these animals round. I felt like they did not need me until I realised they had been issuing me with a stack of IOUs from day one. That beast would have died without my help in calving. That one was stuck and had to be rescued from a mire. We've done this together, and we've rubbed our shoulders.

There is no reason to pass through this place. A tourist might park up and take snapshots here on summer days, but Galloway is not a good place to take photographs. Cameras like contours and busy angles, but this beauty lies in emptiness and the breadth of space. Nobody would ever come to see this blue mass of dark clouds and sighing moorland. You'd need a damn good reason to be out here on a morning like this, and now I have one.

*

Somebody went round to see Sanny and found him gone. It turned out he'd been away at the hospital at Dumfries and he'd died in a ward next to five other men. It was cancer, but he never breathed a word of that to me. You'd never know with Sanny anyway; he could have carried a bear on his back for ten years and never blinked. I looked back and realised that it'd been a while since he'd been round, and then only for short visits.

They opened up the kirk for his funeral. People say it's an ugly old building because it got bombed in the war, but I think it was ugly for years before that. The Germans were trying to wreck the docks at Troon, but they got lost on the way and found themselves flying over a wide expanse of grass and black cattle. They were baffled by that, and they dumped their bombs and never knew they hit the kirk. Old folk say it brought the war home to us. Until that moment, fighting men had gone away and vanished into thin air.

Two dozen men sat and listened to the minister. He gave us a good service, but it was nothing to stir the old regimental flags which hang below the pulpit. These are heavy battle banners scrolled with the names of places in South Africa and India. We used to get around in the old days. Now there's a smell of mothballs and damp velvet. Rooks squalled and circled in the rain, then shiny shoes squeaked like mice as they carried Sanny back outside again. I walked to the car and got the dog out. Sanny always liked that dog, and I held her on a piece of twine as the hearse pulled up. She might have jumped up and scratched the paint, and I almost let her do it because Sanny would've laughed.

Work was done to find his family. A niece came up from somewhere like Northamptonshire to clear out his place. She brought me his fishing kit because he'd left a note saying I needed it. I received bundles of split cane rods and tall stacks of fly-tying equipment, enough to keep me busy the rest of my life. Some of the boxes had flies that Sanny had made – local favourites like grouse and claret, snipe and green, the goat's toe. I wished I'd paid more attention to his fishing advice.

Hardly a week passed before I leant on Sanny and found him gone. I was puzzling with some problem and thought, 'Here's one for Sanny.' A blush of realisation; a new and unlived absence. Now I have lists of things I wish I'd asked him; many will never be answered. And worse, I can't remember some of the answers he gave me.

Now there are only three lights we can see at night-time, and a For Sale sign nods in the cold wind. I saw the house listed in the estate agent's window in Dalbeattie, the place where retired English people come to hunt for holiday homes. There's free health care in Scotland and money just goes so much further, so the houses lie empty for nine months of the year and the young folk say there's nowhere to live.

I'd learned so much from Sanny, but the real value was the whole man. To him, the world was vast and indestructible, and he saw himself blowing around in it like a mote of dust. You could smash that quarry and plough that hill and never heed the fallout because even your grandest deed is tiny beside the scale of a planet. Drain the fields and the birds will just go somewhere else; burn your trash and the poisonous smoke will rise to the infinite sky and be gone.

Sanny and Wullie and my grandfather were born to be tragic heroes. They were the last of a long line of powerful men which runs far back into the ancient forests. They were locked in a fight between progress and nature; it's no wonder I made them into tigers and gods. Their struggle was grim and epic, and it was so clearly doomed to failure that winning caught them off guard. After centuries of creeping progress, we suddenly leapt up and grabbed the world by its throat. I feel weak and mousy in the wake of those men, but I've inherited more power than all of them combined. Nothing can ever be taken for granted again.

*

And all this at the height of our treatments in Glasgow. The nurse said I could be present during the implantation of my wife's fertilised egg. It was hard to imagine what I would bring to the moment, but the process had been so thoroughly scoured of all humanity that it was hard to blame them for trying to rediscover some shred of romance. If the process works, I'll be able to get drunk at Christmastime and embarrass my child with the story of the night he or she was conceived. I'll decide in the spur of the moment whether or not to mention the strip lights and the presence of five other folk.

I don't know if the doctors can help us. There's no ready explanation for our predicament; we're fit and willing, and this could have happened to anyone. I find it too easy to hide in hard work, and then I'm caught unawares and I'm shattered by my failure. For a while the anger and sadness welled around the problem and expressed itself in other ways like a leak. I raged at the cattle and their tragedies crushed me. Like a child, I didn't know that sadness can come in disguise. I couldn't fathom why simple failures stirred such misery.

But then the treatment became its own challenge. You can focus on appointments and injections, and you can feel like you're making progress with every step. The doctors give you a million little goals and you work towards every one. You need the right womb thickness and hormone levels, and there's always more blood to extract and sample. You're asked to tick off the checklist and follow every protocol and you feel like the baby will come at the end like a prize. But even if they pull it off, you're just where everyone else begins. There's still a very long, very chancy pregnancy to endure. I was maddened by how slowly the treatments lugged along. Skip a month and then wait three because the diary's full, and life just ebbs on by and you still don't have a child to take home, and that's not fair because you've given them everything they asked you for.

Maybe this treatment will work. Maybe we'll never have a child. I don't know what's coming. The important thing is these years which have passed in the meantime. I found the first grey hair on my head last Christmas, a landmark of its own. I squirm to think how close we came to squandering this time in stagnant suspense. Some couples save a layer of their wedding cake to eat at the christening. I'm glad we ate ours when it was fresh.

And now I wonder if I'd have the energy to start a farm again from nothing. There was so much work in the early days. I'm surprised by all we did. I can't imagine how this time might have played without the cattle and these thin acres. I've cast off great weights of the past, and now the future is lighter and less important.

*

The bull came home to rest. He'd done his work on the hill but the thrill of it had stripped him back to the bones. I could feel the bumps in his back, and there was a hollow scoop in his side where his belly should have been. We fetched him in to the yard and he slouched around the sheds and the nearby paddocks. One of last year's steers came to keep him company, and they were idle and slack like louts. But it was good to have them home and fine to stare over their backs at the distant cows on the hill. They had no use for him anymore; they wintered out in the whins with their freshly sown bellies. They don't need to be pampered like he does.

The bull was at a loose end, so I reached for the summer oats. We'd kept 200 sun-dried sheaves to wait in the sheds and the mice were rustling their skirts with impatience. Here was the cream of the summer and it was dished out to the dripping boys when the long nights came. Birds hung around their wooden trough, and small finches swirled around those blokes like mosquitoes. Just as I was the man who cut this crop in sweat and short trousers a few months back, it was I who cowped the sheaves and slit them open beneath rakes of bleeding rain and the black ruts of winter mud. It's one hell of a job, this. The boys ate the whole sheaf, straw, chaff and oats together. They munched the stems right down to their butts, and the din of their jaws was a lasting treat.

And then we finished the sheaves and I turned to the sacks of clean grain. We had more than a ton, and every oat had been worked by hand. We could have fed them direct, but oats have a waxy husk and it helps to grind them up into porridge. I found a machine to do this job; I rescued it from a farm beyond Dalbeattie. Not many people have bruisers now, and the mighty contraption was free to a good home. I climbed in the rafters to dismantle the old hoppers and found that somebody had pinned their fag packets in a neat line along the wormy beams. And there were pin-up girls stapled to the wood, winking slyly. The date said 1952, and my first instinct was still to take them home. But they fell apart like ash when I pulled out the staples, and I had my knuckles gently rapped.

The bruiser was a knuckle-busting brute from the 'Albion' works of Messers Harrison and MacGregor in Leigh, and we nearly crapped our puddings in moving it. Sparks sprayed from the trailer axles as we came through the town, and the feet rubbed their way into the steel floor. The machine was older than my father, but then the weight was in place and the belts were tight and ready.

We ran this bruiser by a shaft through a hole in the wall to the tractor. Making that hole was a day's work in itself, and many a tough-tipped drill bit was buggered as we battled the old granite. Then I reversed the tractor and plugged the two machines together. I dropped the clutch and heard the bruiser wheels begin to rumble again for the first time in decades.

I ran a sack of oats through that contraption. The grains were fed into a hopper and rushed out from the heavy wheels in light and waxy flakes. The whole place smelled like porridge to make your mouth water. The sheds shuddered and drummed with the row of heavy wheels, and the tractor puttered on outside, coughing up a thin stream of blue smoke into the cloud. I'd found a way to make history pull its weight; we turned a ton of meal that afternoon.

Then the bull fell upon it and raked his tongue through the crumbly stuff. It made a paste on the roof of his mouth, and he jockeyed for the best slot at the trough. He bubbled and belched, and he ate more and growing mounds of it over the coming days. The birds came to tidy the mash from his feet, and still he stashed it until his back began to swell and the curve of his neck rose up again in the half-dark. I would go to him at dawn when it was light enough to see and then I'd save his evening meal for the last hum of dusk; always him and always here. He could be idle and weak in the slumping days of winter, but instead he's a champion and his fitness shines. I look at him and see my summer's work spelled out in flesh.

It's true what Sanny used to say: 'There's nocht finer than a geed gallowa bull.'

*

The storm was so loud by midnight that sleep had become impossible. I stared at the dark ceiling and began to worry. Every possible disaster ran through my mind, and I pictured dawn breaking on a shattered farm.

Unable to rest and unable to stop worrying, I headed downstairs in my pyjamas and put on a heavy overcoat. I touched the door handle and the door blasted open and slammed a hole in the plaster wall. A cold wind rushed inside and thumbed through a pile of newspapers by the stove. A stack of receipts fluttered onto the ground and danced their chronology into chaos. The only way to save the house was by closing that door behind me.

This is my home. I'm always here, in daylight and darkness. The buildings had become a living comfort, but that wind filled the yard with suspicion and malice. All was not well, and I felt the change with a swell of discomfort. My imagination sparked into life as I crossed back over the yard. Every dark space was filled with clasping hands and silent, staring faces. Muscular winds rubbed the grass into agony, and I stumbled on my heels. Discomfort became a yellow surge of fear – the wind rode over sense and reason and then rose to a scream, a blare of overwhelming noise in the darkness. My clean, steady torchlight was confused with flecks of ice and cold sleet which stung my head and made my knuckles raw.

The cows were out on the hill and would ride this wind like corks in the tide. But I feared for the bull and his pal because they sometimes lay in the doorway of the shed and anything could fall or clatter down on a night like this. So I ran to check them as the wind swirled and burred the puddles in the yard. And they were in the shed right enough, but they were both curled up and dozing like cats. That peace felt deathful and macabre, like sleepers in a burning house; I wanted to waken them and share the panic.

In marching back and forth, I found a flood beneath the rain. A crucial drain had blocked and the water rose in a dark, treacly pool. Without relief, this water would climb up over the step and pour into the hayshed. That gentle summer's hay could be spoiled in a few hours. I was suddenly glad to find some justification for my fears. And there was something I could do to help. I waded in and felt the weight of the water on my boots, a sluggish pull which swirled thickly around my shins and left me covered in shreds of yellow chaff.

I raked the dark water with a wooden shank, digging for the blockage and the rungs of the rusty grate. Ice whipped my hair and clawed at my coat, and then my torch fell in a single turning flash, down into the water as the slates rattled and the sheets of tin roared.

There was a strange yellow glow in the drain for a moment before the batteries drowned. Then utter darkness. The lights in the house rushed far away across the yard, fighting their own battle against the night. They flickered twice as the wind dashed through the overhead wires, and I jabbed the grate until I could feel the water being pulled down into the drain. All this work was fevered by every conceivable spunkie and ghoul pouring into my ears like the wind; horrors mounded themselves around me like drifting snow. I racked my brain for something positive and found only bitterness in the heart of my home. Where were the swallows now? And the deep summer stillness – warm stones, cut grass and daylight? This was no home to me, no place I knew, this wet, hellish misery of ice and darkness and a relentless baffling wind, a wind with nails and teeth and no love for me.

I could have cried aloud, and the wind flayed me then, peeling back a loose sheet of tin from the roof behind me. A whirling hessian bag slapped me in the thigh and I was instantly soaked. The bending stem of an ancient Scots pine was picked out against the sky, flexing like an old man's arm, writhing and working itself apart with every sickening bow until the sinews cracked.

And even when the drain was clear and I was safely indoors, the wind ran ragged round the house and shuffled the slates as if they were playing cards; and always the howl of quickness through narrow places – a dark, miserable whistle like a surge of despair in the night. The electricity had failed, and a candle showed me where the draughts ran like mice round the kitchen. Panes of glass flexed in the wind and the putty cracked with the sound of a chewing insect. I'm a man of thirty-three and I was sorely rattled.

But morning came in peace. I stared out of the window and tried to find some evidence of the night's riot. The world wasn't broken, and the only trace of the storm was a feed bag snagged on the fence below the garden. Nothing had changed, but that yard was no longer mine.

I'd been overfamiliar and presumed to know this place. I'd presumed to know this place. But even when the swallows came home months later and the yard was filled with their fun, that darkness stayed with me and held me at arm's length again. It'll take a lifetime to call this place my own.

*

We went to look at cattle which came up for sale privately. The farmer had taken to his bed, and we were told that the whole place would soon be up for sale. He'd once kept a thousand acres of moorland near Monybuie, but declining years forced his stocking back to a dozen black Galloway cattle, including a fine young bull. Weak, tired and unable to keep up, the farmer had failed to register his animals for several years, and they lacked any form of identification, tags or passports.

This was bad news. Everything has to be traceable nowadays, and animals like these are usually shot on site and their bodies taken to the knacker's yard. There are some ways to launder them back into the system again: unregistered beasts can never be moved, but there's a way to tag their calves and some of the value can be salvaged. These nameless beasts would be cheap to buy because of that legal wrinkle. I was hardly in the market for black cattle, but the right animals might be worth it.

My father and I went out of interest. The track took us three miles up a lonely hillside on a warm evening in May. We came round a final bend and the farm stretched out to the rough horizon. I saw the white-washed farmhouse beneath a stand of Scots pines. The fields dropped down into a low glen where a colony of black-headed gulls churned noisily in the evening light. The car's engine fell to silence and cuckoos pulsed through the open window, an incessant drone which ran without interruption for the hour of our visit. Curlews sang in the breeze above a stirring sea of cottongrass and lambs moaned.

The farmer wasn't fit to see us. He shouted down the stairs, and we could see his house was coming down about him. The walls were black with mould and the wallpaper peeled back like dead skin. We walked through the yard past rotten, empty kennels and out to the back fields where a hare sat and washed his breast in a blue bed of forget-me-nots and speedwell.

The cattle were rough and wild. I could smell the bull's sweat on him, and he rolled his eyes and kept us at a wary distance. The cows were of all ages, and it was odd to see them black and pure without yellow tags or signs of humanity. They were animals of the old breed, thick and short-legged, and they tossed their heads as we leant on the dyke and looked them over. Curlews sang on, and the scene was backed by a dull, washed-out sunset which played over a ten-mile view of deep moss and rough, broken country. It was the old world made new for a few heady moments.

They were fine beasts, but they were wild. It'd be hard to justify my work and travel to keep tame animals, let alone loose and frantic ones. My heart broke for the bull, a fine, stocky gentleman. The wind rippled up the brown fringes on his shoulders and hips, but I hardly had use for him – he would take so much work. Water trickled all the while, and it clicked through a web of burns and drains like the busted capillaries on an old man's face. Stacked clouds piled up in the north, and the curlews turned and went back into the deep grass.

I never went back to that place, but I heard that the beasts were shot where they stood and the bill was passed to the farmer's estate when he died. The land was sold and the fields were planted with commercial forestry because it's the only way to make money on rough ground like that. There are no more curlews there, but I stood alone as the sun set and I stole something from that place; a moment of pure connection when all the riot and snarl of the world fell away to nothing. Small crystals of rock in the dyke top glide below my fingers. They baffle the sun and glitter between scabs of dry moss and lichen. I smell the warmth on the dry grass and my own shadow gabbles in a pool of nettles. There's a curlew singing, and for a moment I know nothing more than that bird in this place. It's the merest moment of wholehearted peace, but I park my fears and I'm suddenly glad that I ever knew these birds at all. The song bores into me, and the cattle stand and toss their tails because maybe they know what I've found.

I left a tall mound of my own grief in that place, and it was buried when the forest ploughs came. I still grieve for Galloway, but I can almost bear that weight now. I'm more canny in the way I use this place, and I've learned to glean goodness wherever I can find it. I pack my belly with things that nobody else will want, and I turn them into gold. Even when the last hills are gobbled and paved, I can carry forward some distillation of an old truth.

December

In dire fettle and foundering, I push up through the broken ground to find altitude. This is an act of desperation in a bleak moment; the hill always provides a shift of perspective and leaves me smiling and renewed. I hope that height will bring clarity, but now the tall ground is dark and cloud-bound, and the grass is threshed in eddies like foam. Night will soon come, and small birds rush away like flecks of spit.

There is no cheap comfort on this hill, but it's a relief to be alone. I love to fly through this country and follow thin tracks through the deep grass. When friends come with me, I chafe and stamp at their slowness. Streaks of this land have grown thick and coarse with white grass which crowds in tussocks like an army of busbies. Newcomers stumble and quickly tire, and of course I wait and say I don't mind, but all I want is to pound through this stuff at a loping jog, hunchbacked and alone.

Rain comes and twilight tows the wide horizon into a single line. Two miles from home and still outbound, I stop and feel the sweat prickling my back. Sheep recoil in horror as if I were some blood-hungry beast in their midst.

Clouded and dark with frustration and gloom, I swear at them for their panic. Vague wings pass overhead, and then comes the onset of twilight, still bounding over grass and scored with flecks of ice and rain which soak through my trousers and drive the blood into my face. It's a miserable damn place on the edge of day when all life has gone away and even the birds are scared to steep their feet in the moss pools. Snot trails on the beak of my nose and then blows away or is trailed in long, streaking tracks up my cuff.

Geese move on the edge of the last light; new birds rumble in the clouds. There is always something coming or going from this place, but these tidal tilts can leave me feeling lumpen and immobile. I am the only constant in a world of shifts and relays.

I can hardly grudge the freedom of birds, but it's an uncomfortable balance to my own static life, squatting on the same few acres like a toad under a stone. And I impose that jail upon my cattle, which would soon move away if they could. But I ring them in with dykes and wires and keep them as my prisoners, and I shatter their dreams for soft grass and mild living. My ancient ancestors would follow their herds around the seasons in a gradual, steady revolution. Those folk were not from Galloway as I am – they had a claim on all the grass from Glasgow to Liverpool. Maybe they would think it was odd to stand all year in the same glen, enduring.

I turn for home and the fading coast. Long gone are the fine days when this place is a balmy, barefoot cushion of skylarks and dusty moss. Gone too is that brief moment in autumn when this grass comes up peachy and red and the rowans are bent with berries. Now the hill is grey and blue and there is nothing but granite and the bones of a sinking tide. Even in the pits of grim bother, I find comfort in my unnatural loyalty.

And now I stand by the dark merse and feel the land moving beneath me. The banks are being undercut by rushing currents, and the mud marches away into the sea. This old bend has moved in the time I've known it, and the steep banks are carved by bubbling tides.

A few white cottages blink on the shore, then there's heather and the first shocks of rain. There's no need to recall this moment above any other. A cool wind comes up from the sea and it runs into the hills as if they were something new.

Acknowledgements

There are many sound and authoritative books on Galloway's history. This is not one of them.

Native has been worked up from a thousand conversations over a fifteen-year period, so perhaps it's no surprise that the result should occasionally wander from certifiable truth. But if folk tell a story about themselves and their place for long enough, then surely that becomes a thing worth hearing.

If I've failed to deliver on 'fact', then I must recognise the value of fiction. It feels important to record my debt to the Victorian writer S.R. Crockett, who spun the folklore and traditions of old Galloway into a series of novels more than a century ago. When I was twelve years old, I read his book *The Raiders* and knew beyond all certainty that I came from a grand and mighty place. The tale of thieves on the Black Water belongs to Crockett's imagination, as does my absolute faith in the power of belonging.

Of course this book could never have been made without the help and support of my wife and our friends, who endured many of these highs and lows with deep and lasting patience. Thank you.

Thanks are also due to my agent, Jenny Brown, who backed *Native* from the beginning, even when it lay in pieces. And from Jenny to the team at Birlinn, particularly Hugh Andrew and Anita Joseph, who stirred the pot at crucial moments.

Finally, I can do no more than nod in deference and respect to the many men who became Sanny. Some, but not all of these, are Joe, Jackie, George, Bill and the gentleman Peter Kelly, who lived all his days at Laggan o' Dee.

They're all away now. We walk in their wake like weakling kids.

Patrick Laurie
March 2020